Introduction

by Steve Clark

This bulletin draws together the major reports by SWP leaders and the resolution adopted by the Socialist Workers Party on the Nicaraguan revolution. It traces the development of the SWP's discussion and views, as the party closely followed the actions of the workers' and farmers' government in Nicaragua and its leadership, the Sandinista National Liberation Front (FSLN).

Included in this bulletin are:

1. "The Nicaraguan Workers' and Farmers' Government and the Revolutionary Leadership of the FSLN," a report by SWP National Secretary Jack Barnes to the November 1979 World Congress of the Fourth International;
2. "The Coming Showdown in Nicaragua and the Tasks of the Fourth International," a report by Pedro Camejo adopted by the SWP National Committee on January 5, 1980;
3. "Revolution in Nicaragua," a resolution adopted by the SWP National Committee on January 5, 1980; and
4. "The New Rise in the World Class Struggle," a report by Steve Clark adopted May 24 by the SWP National Committee. This report includes an evaluation of the deepening of the Nicaraguan revolution during the first five months of 1980.

The central political thread running through all these documents is the importance for the world socialist movement of the leadership capacities that have been exhibited by the FSLN as proletarian revolutionists. This is particularly significant because it is not an isolated phenomenon, but marks an extension of the revolutionary qualities of a Marxist leadership that the Castro team in Cuba has worked to preserve and develop over the past twenty-one years.

The leaders of the Grenada revolution are also representative of this growing internationalist vanguard, which holds out promise for future advances along the road to a mass working-class international.

Events in June and July 1980 confirm the direction of the Nicaraguan revolution and its leadership developed in this bulletin.

At the July 19 rally in Managua celebrating one year of Free Nicaragua, FSLN leader Daniel Ortega announced the expropriation of huge new tracts of idle land. These are lands that private owners had refused to cultivate themselves or rent out to small peasants.

"It is not possible that while there are peasants who want land to plant," Ortega told the crowd of half a million, "latifundists and big proprietors hold fertile land they are not putting to any use. For this reason of elemental justice these lands will cease to be idle by means of the new agrarian reform law."

This new measure came in response to a campaign against the recalcitrant landowners by the Sandinista-led Rural Workers Federation (ATC). The ATC and Sandinista Workers Federation (CST) also spearheaded the drive for a new law adopted June 11 ordering an across-the-board wage increase of 125 córdobas per month for all workers earning less than 1,200 córdobas per month (10 córdobas= US$1). The CST has answered employer resistance to this new law by launching a "Plan of Struggle," which involves enforcement not only of this wage hike but also of health and safety regulations, vacation and pension payments, and union rights.

As significant as these progressive measures themselves is the role of the mass organizations in fighting for them and then mobilizing the toilers to ensure implementation. This worker and peasant participation is encouraged by the FSLN and by the revolutionary government.

". . . our mass organizations must watch over and work to strengthen the political framework of the revolution," wrote FSLN Commander of the Revolution Carlos Nuñez in a pamphlet being widely circulated in Nicaragua today. And "they must be true instruments for receiving, expressing, and conveying the most pressing demands of the masses," as well.

"This means," Nuñez continued, "that the mass organizations, acting in the framework of the general line of the revolution, must have sufficient right to resort . . . to private criticism, public criticism, utilization of all the communications media, and even mobilizations to demand the measures necessary to guarantee that their concerns are heard."

This reliance on mass participation and responsiveness to worker and peasant initiative on the part of the Sandinista leadership is a source of strength for the Nicaraguan revolution and a confirmation of the revolutionary capacities of the FSLN.

Another decisive source of strength is the Sandinistas' internationalism. This has been demonstrated above all during the past year in Nicaragua's support to the liberation of El Salvador from dictatorship and imperialist domination.

"We are in solidarity and we identify with the just and unstoppable struggle of the heroic Salvadoran people and their search for a new society dedicated to freedom and justice," declared Commander of the Revolution Daniel Ortega at the July 19 anniversary rally.

The Sandinistas have been trained and tempered in the school of the class struggle, always striving to learn from their experiences and move forward. But they have also had another invaluable teacher—the Cuban leadership, which has been tested not only in a successful battle for power, but by twenty-one years of leading a revolutionary workers' government under intense imperialist pressure.

The Sandinistas acknowledged this contribution to their struggle by inviting Fidel to be the featured guest at the July 19 celebration. He gladly accepted, but assured the rally, "We do not come here to teach or to influence. We came humbly to learn and be influenced. . . . Just as we are also certain that your example will extraordinarily influence the rest of Latin America."

Revolutionary Cuba has already been in the vanguard of political and material solidarity with Nicaragua, and Fidel again pledged July 19, "We are ready to give you all of our support, all the solidarity of our people without conditions and without advice."

At the July 26 celebration in Cuba a week later, after Fidel's return, FSLN leader Jaime Wheelock explained two other decisive ways in which the Cubans had aided the victory of the Nicaraguan revolution. He said that "the support and advice of our brother Fidel" had helped make possible the reunification of the three divided tendencies of the FSLN, and that the Cuban government had provided in the last weeks leading up to the insurrection the "concrete solidarity" needed for the military victory over Somozaist tyranny.

Assistance and advice from abroad, however, cannot make a revolution, no matter how generous the aid or good the advice. That takes leadership.

And as Fidel explained in Managua July 19, the Sandinistas were victorious because they "managed to pull the entire people behind them. They are the vanguard, not because they want to give themselves the title of vanguard, but because they learned how to win for themselves the place of vanguard in the history and in the struggles of their people."

August 19, 1980

The Nicaraguan Workers and Farmers Government and the Revolutionary Leadership of the FSLN

by Jack Barnes

[The following report on behalf of a minority of the United Secretariat was presented to the November 1979 World Congress of the Fourth International. The theses on which the report is based are published in the special supplement to *International Press/Inprecor* containing the major reports and resolutions of the world congress. These theses are virtually identical to the resolution "Revolution in Nicaragua" adopted by the SWP National Committe in January 1980 and reprinted in this bulletin; only a few factual points differ due to developments between November 1979 and January 1980.

The vote on this report and on the United Secretariat minority "Theses on the Nicaraguan Revolution" at the World Congress was: 35 for, 71.5 against, 5 abstentions and 1.5 not voting.]

* * *

Revolutions are acid tests. Weaknesses that are underneath the surface are suddenly exposed in the heat of the struggle of great class forces that are outside the control of anyone.

The Nicaraguan revolution precipitated a major split on a world scale among those who call themselves Trotskyists. Some currents reacted to this revolution in a completely sectarian way, placing their own organizational concerns and formal schemas ahead of the interests of the Nicaraguan toilers and the world revolution. These forces included Nahuel Moreno's Bolshevik Faction, which engineered the criminal Simon Bolivar Brigade adventure in Nicaragua; the so-called Organizing Committee for the Reconstruction of the Fourth International; and other sectarian groupings.

Since the leaders of these groups who were also elected leaders of the Fourth International persisted in their maneuvers against the Nicaraguan revolution, its Sandinista leadership, and the Fourth International, we correctly threw them out a few days ago. Now they are giving aid and comfort to the imperialist campaign against Nicaragua by holding rallies against alleged political repression in Nicaragua.

But the Nicaraguan revolution has also precipitated important divisions within the United Secretariat. When the revolution first occurred last summer, we hoped this would not be the case. In early August, a majority of the Secretariat Bureau reached agreement on a statement on the revolution, and a large delegation travelled together to Nicaragua. There, further agreement seemed to be reached, including a common approach toward condemning the Simon Bolivar Brigade adventure and a common political stance toward the necessary measures taken by the FSLN to deal with this problem.

Not long after the Nicaraguan trip, however, differences began to appear. And they center not on the label of workers' and farmers' government. They are over the political approach to this revolution and to its leadership.

On the one hand were those who embraced the revolution, saw its worker and peasant character, recognized the revolutionary qualities of its leadership, sought to learn from it, and reflected this approach in their press and political activity. On the other hand were those who, because of preconceived schemas or parochial concerns, adapted to sectarianism and, to one degree or another, recoiled from identifying with the Sandinista leadership.

At the heart of this discussion today is this political approach to the Nicaraguan leadership. And this is intimately connected to the different approaches in the world movement to the revolutionary Cuban leadership and the current in the Caribbean and Central America that looks to the Cuban socialist revolution and its leadership team.

How our movement approaches this current is decisively important. Because a wrong approach is an obstacle to our very reason for existence—constructing a mass revolutionary proletarian international.

That's the debate that's being opened here today.

The Nicaraguan revolution sent shockwaves throughout the imperialist ruling classes, and they have begun to respond. Just in the few days since we've been here at the World Congress, the imperialists and sections of the Nicaraguan bourgeoisie have made a number of probes. And we can expect many more as the revolution continues to advance and deepen.

At the same time, something totally unplanned and unanticipated is occurring in the United States, precipitated by what happened in an embassy thousands of miles away in Iran. A chauvinist, war-mongering propaganda campaign has been launched by the Carter administration. This will bring to a new stage the battle in the United States for the minds of the American workers, a battle over the *political* capacity of imperialism to use its military power as the ruling class probes to see what possibilities are open to it. And this will have a great deal to do with the coming showdowns in Central America and the Caribbean.

These are the kinds of things we can't predict. We can't predict all the moves of the bourgeoisie, or their reaction to sharpening struggles. We can't predict or control the actions of the masses. And we can't predict all the tactical moves a pragmatic imperialism will make.

There is no single imperialist tactic being used against free Nicaragua. When Washington was surprised by the manner in which the Somoza regime was overthrown and the Sandinistas took power, they backed off tactically from seeking to block the FSLN [Sandinista National Liberation Front] from wielding governmental power. But economic aid was withheld and reactionary imperialist-backed probes, and eventual military action, remain constant threats.

I will concentrate on four basic aspects of what the position of the Fourth International should be on: 1) the nature of the post-July 1979 government; 2) the FSLN leadership, and our attitude towards it; 3) the contradictions that the toilers of Nicaragua inherit and how they are being resolved to move the revolution forward; and 4) our responsibilities from the point of view of the new opportunities opening for building a world party of socialist revolution.

* * *

To understand the character of the government in Nicaragua today, we have to begin with the fact that no one, including the FSLN, anticipated what was going to happen in July. A mass upsurge and insurrection occurred in face of the last-minute attempts of imperialism and a sector of the non-Somozaist bourgeois opposition to block this powerful intervention of the masses, including attempts to get the FSLN to lay down their arms and last-ditch attempts by the Somozaists to hold on when Somoza fled. The scope and power of this mass uprising led to the final shattering and demoralization of the National Guard. In this process, not only was the Somozaist state apparatus smashed, but much of the bourgeois opposition became discredited. Thus, an unanticipated situation faced the FSLN—the leadership of the insurrection—after July 19.

Before July 19 the FSLN leadership thought that the relationship of forces would make it necessary to incorporate a certain number of National Guard units into the new army and police. They were convinced that the provisional revolutionary government that they would participate in would initially be a coalition regime with a substantial bourgeois majority. Such a regime had already been outlined in formal agreements with bourgeois opposition forces.

The First Big Test

But something else happened. The FSLN had another option, thanks to the intervention of the masses. And this was the first big, post-insurrection test facing the FSLN.

They did not set up a bourgeois coalition regime. They took the power and used it to begin the national reconstruction of devastated Nicaragua.

What was this bourgeois regime that they thought would come into being, and that they had agreed to in San José, Costa Rica, only ten days before the insurrectional victory?

It did not center around the proposed five-person junta alone, but this junta combined with a Council of State. The Council of State was not only to share all legislative powers with the junta, but was also to have veto power over any junta decision, to be able to pass any laws of its own with a two-thirds majority, to draft a constitution, to draft electoral laws, to set up the entire judicial structure, and to set up the Interior Ministry and all the police forces of the country.

This Council of State was to have an overwhelming majority of bourgeois forces. Of the thirty-three seats agreed to in the Council of State, between six and nine at maximum were partisans of the FSLN. The bourgeoisie, through their own parties, through the Chamber of Commerce, through organizations of industrialists, through the Catholic hierarchy, would have dominated the government. All were to receive representation with full vote.

But this bourgeois-dominated institution did not come into existence.

In the month to six weeks following July 19, the opportunity appeared for the FSLN to follow another course. And they took it.

There was a bourgeois coalition regime in Nicaragua—on paper. It had been set up in Costa Rica. But it was violently aborted before it came to life.

Instead the FSLN-led junta alone named the ministers. The convocation of the Council of State was repeatedly postponed. Finally it was announced in October [1979] that it would be set up in a number of months, probably in May 1980, but that its original composition was now totally invalid because of the revolution. Its composition would now reflect the preponderant weight of the new mass organizations in Nicaragua.

In the light of this evolution, a debate among partisans of the Nicaraguan revolution opened up over whether the junta rules by a majority vote or unanimous vote. The truth is that it rules by neither. It rules by the relationship of class forces. Three junta members are partisans of the FSLN, two are bourgeois figures. The FSLN controls the interior ministry, the army, the police, the agrarian reform. It leads the mass organizations.

Unlike Cuba in early 1959, the ministers do not form a legislative cabinet; there is no bourgeois president with veto power.

The FSLN-led revolutionary army is not an element of an alternative power outside the governmental framework. Each and every move of the Sandinista army, each and every decision, has been ratified by the government, as have been such moves as setting up INRA [the National Institute of Agrarian Reform], which was done immediately following the insurrection, in the same weeks as the decision to abort the bourgeois coalition regime.

So to understand what happened, it is necessary to realize that before July 19 the FSLN had agreed there was going to have to be a coalition government, to a large degree dominated by the bourgeoisie. This government was going to find itself in a series of contradictions with the rebel army, which the Sandinistas had every intention of holding onto and building. In many ways this would have been similar to what occurred in Cuba for a number of months after January 1959.

But the masses themselves, in the weeks of fury in July, created an entirely unanticipated relationship of class forces and smashed the maneuvers of the imperialists. In the face of the new opportunities this created, the FSLN did something different from what they had planned on doing. And a different governing power came into being.

Revolutionary Measures

The character of this new power, though, could only be determined by what it did. And what it did is outlined in our resolution before you. [See pp. 21 of this bulletin.]

To date, the steps taken by the new government include the nationalization of all the assets of Somoza and his associates; nationalization of domestic banking, and controls on all foreign banking; beginning the agrarian reform under the control of INRA; concentration within the agrarian reform on cooperativism; beginning the organization of the agricultural workers; state control over the export of all cash crops in the countryside; nationalization of land, sea, and air transport; taking over the necessary equipment to give the FSLN one of the two major daily papers in the country and radio and television outlets; the launching of large-scale programs, under conditions of harsh austerity, for education, health, and social security. A bill of rights making the interests of the workers and peasants dominant was proclaimed. And the new government has adopted a firm anti-imperialist and internationalist stance concerning Indochina, the Mideast, and Carter's war moves in the Caribbean. It responded to the coup in El Salvador by immediately and unconditionally supporting the revolutionists and the masses against the new regime.

The FSLN has led the mobilization of the masses, including in large demonstrations, like the one to greet Pham Van Dong and the Vietnamese delegation. On November 7, 100,000 Nicaraguans were mobilized in Managua to honor the FSLN's founding leader Carlos Fonseca, who fell in the struggle, and, de facto, to answer the rightist involvement in the demonstration of 8,000-10,000 to greet the archbishop of Managua that had occurred a few days earlier.

The FSLN-led government set up a centralized Sandinista army. The leadership has taken the most dependable of the fighters in the militias and the guerrilla units and integrated them as the political-military cadres to carry out the necessary job of building up an effective revolutionary army.

At the same time, it has publicly pledged to build broad-based militias. These volunteer forces will be based in the workplaces and will receive professional training.

The organization of the CDSs [neighborhood Sandinista Defense Committees] and the unions has continued. The nationalization of the banks was followed by the nationalization of the insurance companies. A couple of weeks ago, the first imperialist property was hit, with the nationalization of the American and Canadian-dominated gold and other mines. Housing reconstruction has begun.

The list of accomplishments of the new Nicaraguan government is contained in the resolution, so I won't attempt to repeat everything. But the nationwide literacy drive is especially important, not only as a way of eliminating illiteracy—a precondition to expanded workers control—but as a means of carrying the revolution to the countryside and forging a link between the peasantry and the government and urban masses. And as a way of educating revolutionary youth about the real life of the rural toilers. It also plays a role in the organization of the defense of the country against counterrevolutionary forces along the Honduran border.

These are not the type of actions that a Council of State dominated by the Chamber of Commerce, the industrialists' organizations, the Catholic hierarchy, and all the bourgeois parties would carry out.

These are not the initial moves of a bourgeois coalition government in a poverty-stricken, devastated country.

These are the moves of a workers' and farmers' government.

One thing must be very clear. Recognizing that a regime is a workers' and farmers' government is not a matter of praising it or pinning a medal on it. It's not to give it moral credit, if anyone is so arrogant as to believe that can be given from outside. It's not to express certainty that it is foreordained under all circumstances to expropriate the bourgeoisie and become a workers' state. It's to recognize a tendency and a fact, in order better to learn from it and throw our weight in the scales to help the revolutionary leadership move it forward.

There can be a workers' and farmers' government where an objective analysis of the facts would lead to pessimistic conclusions about its capacity to move forward to mobilize the masses to expropriate the exploiters and more and more directly govern. But in any case, it's important to recognize the fact of the existence of a workers' and farmers' government.

The workers' and farmers' government in Nicaragua had its origin in a movement with a radical anti-dictatorial and anti-imperialist political program. The new government has not yet proclaimed the revolution to be socialist, but it has spoken more clearly in class terms than the Cuban leadership did for the first nine months of the Cuban revolution.

The FSLN-led government came to power as a result of popular mass struggle, culminating in a civil war. The FSLN was resolute in combatting bourgeois armed power, disarming it, and calling for the masses to arm themselves, in organizing a revolutionary army to defend the conquests of the masses. It has organized and mobilized the CDSs, the unions, the youth and women's organizations, the agricultural workers, and opened a war on illiteracy in a determined drive to crush counterrevolution and to educate the toilers to govern.

The tendency of the new government is not to attack the masses. Its tendency is to respond to the masses and their intiatives to move forward.

Capacity and Tendency

The determination that the new government is a workers' and farmers' government is not made by measuring the extent of the nationalizations, or the scope of the remaining problems and difficulties, which are very real. As Joe Hansen put it in reference to Cuba nineteen years ago, such a determination is made by the government's "tendency to respond to popular pressures for action against the bourgeoisie and their agents, and its capacity, for whatever immediate reasons and with whatever hesitancy, to undertake measures against bourgeois political power and against bourgeois property relations.

"The extent of these measures," Joe said, "is not decisive in determining the nature of the regime. What is decisive is the capacity and tendency"—as shown by its *deeds*. [*The Workers and Farmers Government* by Joseph Hansen, Education for Socialists, page 4; or *Dynamics of the Cuban Revolution* by Joseph Hansen, Pathfinder Press, page 68.]

Beginning the week of the insurrection, up to the actions it took last week, this new government has acted in just this way. There is no bourgeois coalition government that has acted like this, or *could* act like this.

Confrontations Down the Road

This is neither a bourgeois government nor yet a proletarian government. It's a workers' and farmers' government in a country in which bourgeois property and social relations weigh heavily.

Such a situation is inherently unstable. Class confrontations will arise that will be decisive in determining which way the process will develop. As each one arises, the government throws its weight to resolving it in a proletarian direction—toward socialism—or in a bourgeois direction—toward reversing the toilers' gains. So far the direction in Nicaragua has been unambiguous.

Making this characterization involves a recognition that further decisive challenges for the FSLN are down the road. The same was true in Algeria—our recognition that the Ben Bella regime became a workers' and farmers' government did not imply a guarantee that the FLN would lead the socialist revolution to victory. The same characterization of the Cuban government after the summer of 1959 also did not mean placing confidence in the July 26 Movement, at that stage, to lead the process to culmination in socialist revolution. The Fidelistas at that point did not even claim to be socialist. They denied they were Marxists at the time the government became a workers' and farmers' government.

The process in Nicaragua will either go forward to the establishment of a workers' state, or backward to the overthrow of the workers' and farmers' government and the consolidation of a bourgeois government and the capitalist state. This government will support and lead the masses to establish a workers' state, or it will be eroded, weakened, and overthrown.

But this fact—that the key conflicts will be between the masses and the remaining bastions of capitalist power—does not obviate the fact that the class character of the government is crucial. Its weight in the coming struggles will be decisive. The government is a government that is supported by the masses—and correctly so. It is seen by them as a government that acts in their interests, that can help them move forward. This is a correct perception, not a wrong perception.

Cuba 1959—Nicaragua 1979

It's instructive to compare the new Nicaraguan government to the provisional revolutionary government that was formed in Cuba in January 1959, before the establishment of a workers' and peasants' government. Even those of us who went through the early Cuban experience tend to telescope in our memory the different stages.

The situation in Cuba in the first part of 1959 was, in certain ways, a situation of dual power. But not primarily dual power on a military level. In fact, if we were just referring to two opposed military powers, there wasn't much dual power, because the rebel army was controlled by the July 26 Movement.

The duality was not on the military level, but between two genuine conflicting *political* powers. The government, in which sovereignty and legitimacy on that level resided, acted as a political power, whose course was not in the same direction as the course that began to be charted by the July 26 Movement. The two courses more and more diverged from each other. More and more, the government majority—President Urrutia, many ministers, the judiciary—became an *antagonist* of the leadership of the revolution, both within the government and without, not one of the *components* of the revolution.

To a large degree, then, you had what could genuinely be called dual power, which was solved by the action of the masses and reflected on the governmental level. You don't resolve dual power like this simply by removal of some ministers. The removal of the bourgeois ministers was the reflection of a change in the class character of the government and the class relationship of forces in the country.

What was the real situation in Cuba? At first, the police were virtually unpurged. The first purge of the police didn't happen until the summer and fall of 1959.

The judiciary was relatively unpurged, too. It was *used* by the bourgeoisie to block agrarian reform measures and other changes. While a dual judicial system existed for the few weeks necessary to try the Batista torturers and murderers, the first purge of the judiciary didn't come until November 1959, and then a second one came later. In Nicaragua, the FSLN has prevented the emergence of an independent judiciary that can block revolutionary decisions in spite of the fact that this was called for in the pre-July 19 agreements. Many judicial matters are handled by the FSLN-controlled Ministry of the Interior.

The militia in Cuba was not even proposed until late October 1959. It was set up in the next three months with no effective military training, as Fidel later pointed out, and that was changed only after the Bay of Pigs.

G-2, the secret police, was not in the hands of the July 26 Movement until June 1959, when Ramiro Valdez took over command from a bourgeois army officer. INRA was not even set up until the end of May or beginning of June. There was no July 26-led union organizing efforts until the end of May, when the Humanist Workers Front was set up. There was no union organizing in the countryside until after that, with the setting up of the union structures by INRA.

There was no equivalent of the CDSs, because the victory over Batista did not result from a mass urban insurrection. There was no equivalent to the organization of the CST (Sandinista Trade Union Confederation) and the ATC (Rural Workers' Association). There was no equivalent to the immediate launching of a mass women's organization, or of the organization of a revolutionary youth organization. And the last major bourgeois minister, López-Fresquet, was not even purged until February 1960—many months after a workers' and farmers' government had come into existence in Cuba.

These differences between the early period of the Cuban revolution and the new Nicaraguan revolution do not mean the FSLN is "better" than the Castro team. No. What these differences mean is that in Cuba there was a real conflict, with a real bourgeois coalition government, facing another power center—the revolutionary armed forces, increasingly backed by mass mobilizations. This contradiction and conflict was resolved between June and October, 1959.

This is the opposite of the reality in Nicaragua today.

Character of the FSLN Leadership

On the question of the character of the FSLN and our attitude towards it.

They have one great advantage over the Cubans of 1959—*they stand on the shoulders of the Cubans.*

Their heritage is not just Sandinista, not just anti-imperialist. They were trained, molded, and even carried out faction fights in a framework of looking to the Cubans as the leadership of a Marxist current the Sandinistas were part of.

One cannot read the speeches of FSLN leaders like Carlos Fonseca—speeches in the late 1960s and early

1970s, which have been published and are now circulated in Nicaragua—without seeing the difference in how the FSLN posed class questions, as compared to the positions of the early July 26 Movement.

The FSLN leaders have proven themselves to be revolutionists. They not only responded to pressure from the masses, but they seized the opportunity created by the masses, took power, and have led the way forward.

The coming task will *not* be establishing a workers' and farmers' government. It will be to use this governmental power in dealing definitively with the economic and political power of the bourgeoisie when it is used to obstruct the revolution. In the countryside, this power is symbolized by ownership of cotton and coffee, and in the cities, by bourgeois ownership and control in industry and commerce.

There will be no way of avoiding this confrontation because the bourgeoisie will begin to react to incursions on its prerogatives. *This* is what the confrontation will be about.

Of course, the difficulties facing the revolution are great. The extent of bourgeois ownership, its strength in the countryside, its positions of influence not only in these areas, but through its connections, especially international monetary connections, with its imperialist allies are real. The bourgeoisie also wields a certain amount of de facto, day-to-day, decison-making power through technocrats and in the economic ministries.

At the same time, terrible austerity has been forced upon the FSLN led toilers by the devastation they inherited from Somozaism and imperialism. It would be false, however, to deduce from these objective difficulties facing the revolution that it will be halted or fail. Not at all. It will be the mobilization and organization of the masses, and the capacities of the leadership, that will determine which way the coming conflicts will be resolved.

Neither the imperialists nor the Nicaraguan bourgeoisie are orchestrated by Robelo [one of the two bourgeois members of the junta] or anyone else. The current tactics that imperialism and the "anti-Somoza" national bourgeoisie are using are not permanent. The tactics they try at any one time are one thing. The coming conflicts, in which there will be uncontrolled elements, are another.

The masses will have a decisive say in these confrontations, as well. They will respond. They have joined and are building their mass organizations to respond to challenges from the capitalists. They've been taught by their leaders that this is the purpose of their mass organizations, and they will attempt to use them to further their own class interests. Their actions can even go beyond what the FSLN thinks is possible. The last time this happened, in the insurrection, the FSLN itself responded to the masses.

It is important not to misjudge the stage of the revolution, and therefore misjudge the tasks before it. The government is not the center of bourgeois power, opposed to a center of power of the toilers. To the contrary, the government, as shown by its actions, is *in harmony with* not *in opposition to,* the proletarian direction and tendency of the leadership of what Lenin called a real peoples' revolution.

It is this very fact that poses the following alternative: Either the bourgeoisie must change the government, or its economic power will progressively be crushed and a workers state established.

If you have the wrong position on the government, if you think the new Nicaraguan government is more or less the kind of government that existed in Cuba the first six months of 1959, if you think that kind of conflict is the central contradiction, then you will be wrong on the timing, pace, and ultimately the tasks of the Nicaraguan revolution. You misjudge the leadership; you misorient our members. An increasingly sectarian stance is bred.

Revolutionary Cuba and the Coming Confrontation

A factor that will be decisive to the future of this government is how Cuba will respond to conflicts and confrontations down the road. Those who, unlike me, are pessimistic on this score should feel even more obligated to throw everything into mobilizing defense of the Nicaraguan revolution, because what Nicaragua will face will be awesome if this pessimistic view is correct.

We are being tested in these events like everyone else.

We believe the stakes in Nicaragua are enormous. What is being fought out now is whether or not the socialist revolution in the hemisphere that opened with the Cuban victory will be extended and the second workers' state in the Americas will be consolidated.

A positive outcome of this struggle will have a gigantic impact on Central America, on the Caribbean, on Latin America, on North America. It is inconceivable that this could happen without attempts by Yankee imperialism to stop it from occurring. Regardless of what tactics they use, they will not simply sit back and allow that to occur. Although they are not in good shape given the world relationship of class forces today, the exact political shape they will be in when this showdown happens will be decided in struggle.

We must assume, as the Nicaraguans assume, as the Cubans assume, that the showdown stage of the revolution, which could coincide with the struggle for power in other parts of Central America, will be met by the power of Washington. And in this conflict, Cuban aid will be extremely important.

I'm convinced that the Cubans will come to the defense of Nicaragua when it comes to a confrontation, even war, with American imperialism. I'm absolutely convinced that not only are the masses of Cuba ready to die for Nicaragua, but that the Castro leadership will respond decisively to any United States use of military force. I believe they will do this no matter what Moscow's position is.

The fate of the Cuban and Nicaraguan revolutions are now intertwined. It's too late to separate them. And their intertwining extends toward Grenada, and could encompass El Salvador and Guatemala in the future.

It's important—as the Cubans insist—to recognize that this relation is not a one-way street.

If Nicaragua moves toward greater workers' democracy, and forms of workers participating in governing, toward further development of mass organizations, this will have a powerful impact on Cuba.

If the socialist revolution is extended, it will deepen the revolutionary spirit and atmosphere in Cuba. And if the Cubans have to come to the aid of the Nicaraguans in such an international showdown, it will affect the relationship of class forces on a world scale. It will deeply affect the class struggle in the United States. Because any showdown like this will pose the question of war or peace to the American working class. It will test whether we are correct in what we say about the depth of the antiwar attitudes among American workers.

It will also mean a total new shake-up favorable to building a world movement of socialist revolution.

If a defeat takes place, the consequences will also be enormous.

We're convinced that the stakes are high in Central America. We're convinced that regardless of the exact timing, a showdown cannot be avoided. It must be assumed that imperialism will intervene, and it must be assumed that Cuba will respond. And we must act on that assumption.

This helps explain the deep going internationalism of the Nicaraguan leadership.

Building a World Revolutionary Party

How can we use this opening, meet this responsibility, which the emergence of a new levy of revolutionists onto the world scene offers, to build the world party of socialist revolution?

This is not a new question for us. It's one we've been grappling with and acting on since the emergence of the Castro leadership, an anti-Stalinist revolutionary leadership, two decades ago. But the victory of the Sandinistas marks a major extension of what Joe Hansen—in his 1967 preface to *Che Guevara Speaks*—pointed to as "the rise of a generation of revolutionary fighters. . . . effective leader[s], committed to the socialist goal, whose outlook converged more and more with the classical revolutionary Marxist tradition that stood behind the October 1917 Russian Revolution."

What does this mean for our movement? How must we respond to this opportunity?

We place ourselves with the FSLN leaders, with the militants, with the workers, on the road to reconstructing Nicaragua, to the expropriation of the bourgeoisie and the defeat of imperialism and to the extension of the revolution. That's our common road with them—the elimination of bourgeois power and the defeat of imperialism. Within that common framework we learn, we present our ideas, we apply our program.

Here there is a big difference between the majority resolution and the one I am reporting for. The differences are not mainly about the objective contradictions the revolution faces, on which the two resolutions agree. It's recognizing where the government and where the masses are in the revolutionary process, the character of the leadership, what that means about the coming confrontations, and how we act as part and parcel of that process.

The Fourth International must turn outward toward the Nicaraguan revolution and its revolutionary leadership, away from responding to sectarian pressures, away from narrow preoccupations. If we write a single word in a single resolution because some sectarian accuses us of "liquidating" or not wanting to build a party, that's a betrayal, a dereliction of our duty as revolutionists. We say what we have to say about the Nicaraguan revolution not to answer sectarians, not to cover ourselves in case the FSLN doesn't measure up to its historical responsibilities—and they have measured up just fine so far—but in order to train the cadres of the International as part of the vanguard of the workers of the world on how to move in a situation like this to join with other revolutionists in building an international current capable of moving toward a real mass world party of socialist revolution.

This means approaching this leadership as fellow revolutionists, as fellow revolutionary leaders, who are proving themselves in action and correctly expect us to do the same where we have forces. It means reversing the dangerously sectarian, and ignorant, underestimation of the Castro leadership. It means gladly accepting, rather than resisting, when a chance presents itself not to swim against the stream.

We have to see the Nicaraguan revolution as *our* revolution. *Our* future is deeply involved in the outcome in Nicaragua. It's not just in the United States and Canada, or in Colombia and Mexico, where Nicaragua will have a great amount to do with building the Fourth International, but throughout the entire world.

It was not the Fidelistas or Sandinistas who were riven with sectarian responses to the revolutionary events in Nicaragua—it was the Fourth International. It is not only the Fidelistas and Sandinista leadership who will be tested by the coming events—it is us. They have passed mighty tests; we must recognize this to do so ourselves. If we can do this, if we can *learn* from living revolutions, if we can *act* as revolutionists when the opportunity arises we can play an indispensable role in taking another step toward a mass world party of socialist revolution. This is our challenge and this is our opportunity—the greatest since the founding of the Fourth International.

The Coming Showdown in Nicaragua and the Tasks of the Fourth International

by Pedro Camejo

[The following report was adopted by the National Committee of the Socialist Workers Party on January 5, 1980. The vote was: 37 for, 1 against, 1 abstention, 0 not voting. The consultative vote was: 33 for, 0 against, 0 abstentions, 1 not voting. The resolution "Revolution in Nicaragua" also adopted by the plenum of the National Committee was published in the February 1, 1980, *Militant*. It is included in this bulletin, pp. 21-33.]

* * *

At the heart of the resolution being presented to this National Committee plenum is the recognition that the mass insurrection that triumphed on July 19 of last year so altered the class relationship of forces that the FSLN leadership was able to assume power and quickly consolidate a workers' and farmers' government. The Nicaraguan class struggle since July 1979 has been marked by the organization and mobilization of the worker and peasant masses, while the imperialists and the national bourgeoisie have been retreating, while trying to get themselves in a position to recover lost ground. While the masses, under the leadership of the FSLN, are expanding their organization and deepening their class consciousness, the exploiters are probing for weak points in the revolution so as to be in the best position to block the creation of the second workers' state in the Americas.

The main contradiction in Nicaragua today is the one between the workers' and farmers' government, which rests more and more on the growing mass organizations, and the still-existing, though greatly weakened, capitalist economy, and the limited but real role bourgeois figures still play in the state apparatus and economic organizations.

With decisive state institutions such as the army and police no longer in the hands of the bourgeoisie, the capitalists will not make major investments in Nicaragua. The workers' and farmers' government, on the other hand, in order to maintain the support it enjoys among the masses, must find ways to boost production, create jobs, and implement programs to solve pressing social needs.

This contradiction can be resolved in only two ways. Either the FSLN will use its governmental power to further organize and mobilize the workers, peasants, and urban plebian masses to expropriate, over time, the remaining native bourgeois and imperialist holdings, and consolidate a workers' state that protects and promotes a planned economy based on production for human needs and not private profits. Or else the bourgeoisie will undermine and eventually overthrow the workers' and farmers' government, establish a bourgeois government, reconsolidate the capitalist state, and launch a program of repression and capitalist austerity against the masses. And this, it's now clear, would involve a bloody civil war.

There is no middle road, no third path that can be taken—Nicaragua will either follow the class road taken by Cuba—regardless of concrete differences—and advance towards a workers state, or else will fall back to the restabilization of capitalist rule as occurred in 1965 after the Algerian revolution failed to advance.

The Insurrectionary War and Its Aftermath

Let us look more closely at some of the developments referred to in the resolution.

The Program of Government, which the FSLN, as part of a coalition of anti-Somoza forces, agreed to just before the victory, was not carried out after July 19. Why? Without answering this question it is impossible to explain the dynamics of the ongoing revolution in Nicaragua.

As the Somoza dictatorship became isolated politically and confronted a mass movement using proletarian methods of struggle, the imperialists began to try to resolve the crisis so as to minimize the degree of destruction of the bourgeois state. The U.S. imperialists, the Somozaists, and the anti-Somoza bourgeoisie all recognized the necessity to salvage something of the National Guard in one form or another, since it acted as both police and army for capitalism in Nicaragua. At best, they sought to resolve the crisis by granting political concessions to the masses—reform and purging of the National Guard, some democratic rights, bourgeois-democratic institutions.

As the anti-Somoza forces grew stronger, such concessions required the removal of the Somoza family dynasty. But the Somozas had ruled for more than forty years; it was not so easy to simply remove the dictator and his clique from power. In face of this difficult problem, the anti-Somoza capitalists split over tactics. One wing clung to the increasingly futile perspective of simply negotiating Somoza's exit. Others attempted to use the mass protests and armed revolutionary actions as additional bargaining chips. The latter forces finally associated themselves directly with the radical and plebian elements of the anti-Somoza forces that were seeking the revolutionary overthrow of the dictatorship. They did so in hopes of controlling or moderating the outcome.

On the other side of this bloc, the FSLN was trying to put together the broadest possible united front for revolutionary action. In doing so, it undertook negotiations and made agreements, aimed both at dividing and weakening the bourgeoisie and at gaining concrete aid, especially arms and financing.

Perceptive first-hand, detailed information on the final two years of the struggle is now beginning to appear. We will want to study this material closely so as to more concretely understand the evolution of the process I just described. But most importantly, we do know the results. The masses intervened on a scale seldom seen in the history of Latin America. Unlike late 1958 in Cuba or even in the 1952 Bolivian revolution, an insurrectionary mass movement swept Nicaragua, bringing broad layers of proletarian and plebian youth into an armed uprising that had the active solidarity of the workers, peasants, and large sections of the petty bourgeoisie.

In the course of the uprisings, a popular guerrilla army in the countryside and the cities coalesced around the FSLN's relatively small nuclei of guerrilla fighters. This army battled and demoralized Somoza's National Guard and together with the urban insurrection brought about its total collapse.

In the course of the insurrection the urban masses came onto the center stage of history, altering all the machinations, negotiations, agreements, and plans that others had projected. In so changing the relationship of class forces, the masses opened the way for a solution *in their class interests*.

So this is the first part of the answer to our question—the intervention of the masses. The second part of the answer has to do with the nature of the FSLN as a leadership.

In the concrete circumstances of Nicaragua in July 1979, the only possible political expression the intervention of the masses could take was support to the FSLN—the most radical, intransigent, and committed wing of the anti-Somoza forces. Given this mass support, coupled with the fact that most of the bourgeois oppositionists were discredited in the eyes of the masses, the FSLN found itself on July 19 with military power in its hands.

As students of the Russian Revolution, we know that when the Tsar fell to a mass uprising in February 1917 the majority of the workers and peasants tried to place power in the hands of organizations they perceived as representing their interests—primarily the Mensheviks and Social Revolutionaries, which together held an overwhelming majority in the Soviets. These parties consciously turned governmental power over to the bourgeoisie; they used their influence with the masses to assure the rule of the exploiting minority.

The FSLN did not do this. Many thought it would; many thought it would be forced to. It could have, but it did not. Instead, the FSLN in a matter of weeks took the power into its own hands. When I say power, I mean *political* power, as expressed governmentally and militarily. Another way to express what happened would be to say that the FSLN provided the necessary leadership so that the gains won by the insurrection of the toilers would be consolidated rather than betrayed.

This was expressed in the total destruction of the National Guard and its replacement by a worker and peasant army, and in the replacement of Somoza's government by a government responsive to the needs and interests of the workers and peasants. These key steps were accompanied by a series of social reforms and, most important, the building and strengthening of the mass organizations.

The intervention of the masses and the revolutionary, pro-worker, pro-peasant consciousness of the FSLN were the two ingredients that resulted in the consolidation of a workers and peasants government soon after July 19.

The Original Program of Government

Let's look at the forms this process took.

A program of Government had been agreed to on July 9 in San Jose, Costa Rica, by most sectors of the opposition, including the FSLN. It was published and widely distributed. This program called for a three-part government—a five-member junta; a thirty-three-member, bourgeois-dominated Council of State (which was to draft a constitution and have veto power over junta decisions); and a Supreme Court and judicial system appointed by the Council of State. Not exactly like the U.S. government, but with the same three branches—executive, legislative, and judicial, and the same "checks and balances" to maintain bourgeois domination. Of course, all of this was to be a temporary arrangement followed by elections and the establishment of an elected bourgeois-democratic set-up.

What actually happened?

- The Council of State was postponed until May 1980. It will have a different class character from what was foreseen—it is to be based on the mass organizations of workers and peasants as they have emerged since July.
- Neither the Supreme Court nor any other part of the proposed judicial system is functioning. There is no "independent" bourgeois-dominated judiciary able to check and balance governmental decisions.
- The five-member junta was established. As it turns out, however, the junta has a three-to-two FSLN majority.
- On September 1 the National Directorate of the FSLN declared its nine members to be "Commanders of the Revolution." They are its highest decision-making body.

Without a clearly delineated relationship, it is the junta and the National Directorate that together make up the decision-making power of the present Nicaraguan government. This is an accepted fact—no other executive or legislative body exists; no knowledgeable reporter or commentator on Nicaragua has challenged this description of the regime.

- A new "Statute on the Rights of Nicaraguans" was decreed in August, superseding the Program of Government in many respects and further altering things to the benefit of the masses.

What has this new government done so far? This is outlined carefully in the resolution. To my knowledge no one disputes these facts either. Briefly they are as follows:

- Nationalization of a large part of the economy. We do not know exactly what percentage. These nationalizations include the property of the Somozaists and a bit more.
- Land reform. About 60 percent of the largest farms have been nationalized, representing about 30 percent of all land under cultivation. All debts owed by small peasants have been cancelled, and other measures have been taken to aid this sector.
- A partial monopoly over foreign trade, with a state monopoly on coffee, cotton, and other major agricultural exports.
- Nationalization of the Nicaraguan banks (and state control over imperialist banks) and insurance companies.
- A whole series of social programs including emergency food distribution, a massive literacy campaign, free medical care, rent reductions, and housing construction.
- A clear anti-imperialist foreign-policy stand on the main confrontations taking place in the international class struggle.
- Rapid building of a strong, disciplined, and revolutionary minded army, along with plans for expansion of the popular militias, which will be based in the work places.
- Imposition of price controls, monitored and enforced by the Sandinista Defense Committees.

There is one other thing this government has done that is decisive, in our opinion. *It has helped, rather than obstructed, the organization, education, and mobilization of the masses.*

In Nicaragua the government and the FSLN are not one and the same thing, although there is an overlap. Most of the mass organizing has been done by the FSLN, acting as a revolutionary party in formation. But government actions facilitate this process.

There is nothing so profoundly revolutionary, so profoundly proletarian, as the FSLN's efforts to put the masses in motion, raise their consciousness, strengthen their organization and self-confidence, and organize them to be the driving force of the revolution.

The FSLN's perspective and efforts are in basic harmony with the needs of the masses. The result has been the rapid development of trade unions, whose new leaders think of themselves as *social* revolutionists and not as narrow "trade unionists." The Sandinistas have massively expanded the unions of peasants and farm laborers. They have promoted and developed the neighborhood-based Sandinista Defense Committees. They have encouraged and helped to politicize the organizations of the small oppressed nationalities along the Atlantic coast, such as the Miskitos, Sumos, and Ramas. And out of the most resolute and self-sacrificing layers of the young workers and peasants they are building a new army, militia, and police.

In all this organizing activity, the FSLN promotes class consciousness. It teaches the workers that they are a revolutionary vanguard class; that capitalists are exploiters and that the Sandinista revolution will end all exploitation. They teach the soldiers, *milicianos,* and police that they are the armed forces of the toiling masses; that they exist to fight imperialism, to fight against oppression and inequality.

Workers' and Farmers' Government

Why do we recognize the present Nicaraguan government as a workers' and farmers' government? What are our criteria?

First, we recognize that the bourgeoisie has lost control over the government. The government is taking measures in the interests of the workers and peasants. This is demonstrated concretely in its actions, in its willingness to challenge bourgeois property and political prerogatives.

A workers' and farmers' government is a government that is neither definitively bourgeois nor as yet definitively proletarian. In his initial document in the SWP's 1960 discussion on Cuba, Joseph Hansen characterized a workers' and farmers' government as "a highly contradictory and highly unstable regime, subject to pressures and impulses that can move it forward or backward."

Joe went on: "By recognizing the new Cuban government as a workers' and farmers' government, we indicate its radical petty-bourgeois background and composition and its origin in a popular mass movement, its tendency to respond to popular pressures for action against the bourgeoisie and their agents, and its capacity, for whatever immediate reasons and with whatever hesitancy, to undertake measures against bourgeois political power and against bourgeois property relations. The extent of these measures is not decisive in determining the nature of the regime. What is decisive is the capacity and the tendency."

Hansen also stated succinctly the tasks revolutionary Marxists propose for such a government and what our attitude should be towards it. He recalled the tasks of a workers' and farmers' government outlined in the "Theses on Tactics" adopted by the Fourth Congress of the Communist International: ". . . to arm the proletariat, to disarm bourgeois counter-revolutionary organizations, to introduce the control of production, to transfer the main burden of taxation to the rich, and to break the resistance of the counter-revolutionary bourgeoisie." As for our attitude, Hansen said: "Insofar as such a government takes practical measures against the bourgeoisie—that is, begins to resolve its contradictory position in the direction of socialism—it warrants support. And insofar as it grants democratic rights to revolutionary socialism, it warrants a fraternal attitude. Against imperialism, it must, of course, be supported unconditionally." [All quotes from "The Character of the New Cuban Government," contained in Joseph Hansen's *Dynamics of the Cuban Revolution* (New York: Pathfinder, 1978), pp. 65-72.]

What exists in Nicaragua is a government that is in fact carrying out the tasks described by the Comintern resolution, as well as several more. The economy today is partially in the hands of the state; an important part remains in the hands of the bourgeoisie. Increasing limitations have been placed on the bourgeoisie's economic power through governmental decrees and the development of workers' control, but the class character of the *state*—that is, the property relations as yet *permitted* by the repressive forces (if less and less defended by them)—remains, on the whole, capitalist. The masses are mobilizing and coming into conflict with the existing capitalist economic order. The interests of one or the other must triumph in relatively short order. In broad terms, this is a description of the present conjuncture in Nicaragua.

Dual Power?

The resolution on Nicaragua adopted by a majority of the delegates at the recent World Congress of the Fourth International suggested that the current situation might best be described as a "special kind of dual power." [See "Revolution on the March" in the special supplement to *Intercontinental Press,* January, 1980.] The supporters of this position hold that although the FSLN is predominant in the government, conflicting class forces compete in determining governmental policies. In their view, it is wrong to recognize one class force or another—the bourgeoisie or the workers and peasants—as predominant. So they simply place the label "dual power" on Nicaragua. The government, they say, is a "coalition with the bourgeoisie" but not a bourgeois government or a workers' and farmers' government. Thus we are faced with a government that has been in place for five months but has no class character.

What is worse, these comrades fail to explain, except in vague and general terms, where the two different conflicting governmental authorities are to be found under these conditions of "dual power." The two counterposed powers have no names or addresses.

I want to raise a few considerations on why the Political Committee thinks that acting on the belief that the situation in Nicaragua today is one of dual power is not only inaccurate but is disorienting as to the current stage of the revolutionary process in Nicaragua and can therefore lead to placing emphasis on driving a supposed "bourgeois pole" out of the government.

First, we should understand that we *are* describing a situation where there is a "duality of power" of a certain kind. The capitalists retain important economic power. This fact inevitably influences the political decisions of the government and affects various public institutions. Yet the class interests of the workers and peasants are predominant in determining the policies of the government. They control the army, police, and militia. The workers and peasants present a growing force through their new political and economic mass organizations and mobilizations. Most importantly, the decisions of the government have led to less power, not more, in the hands of the bourgeoisie. And they prepare the workers to govern directly.

Each of these contending class camps has important international allies that enter into the relationship of forces. The capitalists enjoy the backing of imperialism, with its overwhelming economic and military power. They also have the support of the national bourgeoisies of the other Latin American countries.

The workers and peasants also have international allies. Revolutionary Cuba is an ally both objectively and concretely in day-to-day aid and support. The toiling masses also enjoy substantial international solidarity, especially among their counterparts elsewhere in Latin America and to a lesser degree in sectors of the proletariat of the imperialist countries. They receive diplomatic support and some economic aid from most of the workers' states.

The petty bourgeoisie within Nicaragua is divided. The upper strata generally support the bourgeoisie and the lower sections lean towards the proletariat.

So two antagonistic class forces confront each other, each with its specific base of power. But these bases of power are not embodied in two opposed centers of governmental power or two opposed armies, or a counterposed government and army each trying to subvert the other. Prior to July 19, there was a short period when two governments and armies did face each other, but the insurrectionary victory ended that dual-power situation.

The FSLN's predominance reflects the bourgeoisie's loss of control over the government. The majority resolution does not contend that the bourgeoisie controls the FSLN or any section of its National Directorate. That individuals within the FSLN leadership may still be responsive to bourgeois pressures is another matter. It is also true that two of the five junta members are bourgeois figures. But that alone neither constitutes dual power nor reveals the class character of the government.

Precisely because the government is independent of the bourgeoisie while the latter retains important economic power, the correct way to characterize the basically unstable situation is a workers' and farmers' government in a capitalist state operating within fundamentally capitalist property relations. To call it dual power would imply the existence of two counterposed centers of governmental power and, at least potentially, two rival military forces within Nicaragua.

And to call it a "very special kind" of dual power embodied in a government of indeterminate class character offers no greater clarity. All workers' and farmers' governments that we are familiar with have come into being during periods of intense class struggle in which one could say that very special kinds of duality of power exist.

Fortunately, there are historical examples that can be cited to shed more light on this problem. We can look back at how we analyzed similar situations in the past. Parallels and differences with Cuba are most familiar and were discussed at the World Congress. Here I want to take up two other examples that were not mentioned at the World Congress or referred to only in passing—China and Algeria.

These two cases are useful because in each one a strong argument could have been made to characterize them as situations of dual power. But in each case the Fourth International found it more accurate at a certain stage to recognize the existence of a workers' and farmers' government and a state still marked by capitalist property relations.

China

In 1952 the International Executive Committee of the Fourth International held a discussion on the character of the government then in power in China. The IEC correctly decided to reject the characterization of "dual power" and instead recognized that a workers' and farmers' government had come into being. One could have made a much more convincing argument for the dual power characterization than in the case of Nicaragua today. The bourgeoisie was still entrenched in the government in the south of China. Major bourgeois figures held posts in the central government, and a certain amount of armed resistance was going on against the land-reform measures.

Comrade Ernest Mandel, who was the reporter for the majority at the 1952 IEC plenum put it this way: ". . . we think that it is more prudent and more correct to stop at this point for the moment, to acknowledge the elements of dual power which still remain in China today, to characterize the government *therefore* as a workers and peasants government which has in practice already broken the coalition with the bourgeoisie . . ." ["Report and Discussion on the Third Chinese Revolution," Education for Socialists Bulletin, *The Workers and Farmers Government.* Emphasis added.]

Explaining further why the term "dual power" was not useful, Mandel added in his summary: "On the level of the central government, two governments do not confront each other in China, as was the case in Russia, or in Germany in 1918, or in Spain, at least in an embryonic form, in 1936." (It should be noted that today Comrade Mandel holds the "dual power" position regarding Nicaragua.)

Algeria

We also had the experience of the Algerian revolution in the early 1960s. Again, in comparison with Nicaragua, one could have made a stronger case for the existence of dual power. As in Nicaragua there was a famous group of nine leaders of the Algerian National Liberation Front. But unlike in Nicaragua the FLN leaders were openly divided between those who supported the capitalists and those who based themselves on and sought to act in the interests of the workers and peasants. The military was also divided between regional sectors whose leaders favored one side or the other. Houari Boumedienne—who eventually toppled the Ben Bella government—led a section of the military, built outside Algeria's borders, that had taken no major part in fighting the French and that vacillated between the two contending sides.

When under the pressure of the masses the Algerian government of Ben Bella responded to the workers and peasants and took important measures against capitalist property and political power, the Fourth International recognized it was a workers' and farmers' government, not a situation of dual power.

So if the case could be made for the existence of workers' and farmers' governments in China and Algeria, where it was generally recognized that elements of dual power did exist, then certainly this characterization is by far the most accurate and politically correct one for Nicaragua—precisely for the reasons that Ernest Mandel cited in reference to China: the nonexistence of two central governmental powers, or two military forces, confronting each other inside the country.

I might add that our assessment flows from the fact that the military is wholly under the control of the FSLN, that the FSLN is so predominant in the government, that there are not contradictory policy decisions made (as there were during much of 1959 in Cuba before the consolidation of a workers' and farmers' government), and that the FSLN is made up of revolutionists of action who not only consider themselves Marxists seeking to act in the interests of the workers and peasants, but who actually organized and took power by revolutionary means.

Profound differences exist between us and those groups outside the Fourth International that call themselves Trotskyist while claiming that the FSLN is carrying out a class-collaborationist line and that Nicaragua thus has a bourgeois government. We will take this question up at more length later.

Nicaragua and Cuba

Now let us look at the Nicaraguan process in comparison to the way the Cuban revolution unfolded. This will aid us in discussing the most important aspect of this report—the coming showdown in Nicaragua.

The first thing we should note is the difference between the struggle to overthrow Somoza's dictatorship and the one that brought down Batista's in Cuba. As we noted earlier, the Nicaraguan masses were organized and involved in the military fight to a much greater degree than was the case in Cuba. Added to this is the FSLN's considerably higher political consciousness as compared to that of Cuba's July 26 Movement at the outset.

The fact that Somoza and his National Guard held out much longer and utilized more of their firepower against the mass insurrection than did Batista and his henchmen means that the Nicaraguan economy suffered far greater damage in the revolutionary war. While the Cubans triumphed with virtually all the island's industry, commerce, and agriculture intact, the Nicaraguans face gigantic tasks of reconstruction. Even aside from the war damage, Nicaragua is less developed economically than Cuba was in 1959, and the urban proletariat of Nicaragua is considerably smaller than was Cuba's.

As a result of these and other factors, the Nicaraguan process has not followed a path identical to the Cuban one. Nicaragua did not go through a phase during which a bourgeois coalition government made contradictory moves and set up structures that later had to be dismantled, as happened in Cuba under Urrutia and Miró Cardona. Instead a workers' and farmers' government was consolidated within a matter of weeks.

We can list other differences between Nicaragua and Cuba. Among the most important are the following:

- The Sandinista Defense Committees (CDS) grew directly out of the organization of the masses before and during the insurrection. The CDSs are already being centralized and have begun taking on governmental responsibilities, above all on the municipal level. But in Cuba the Committees for Defense of the Revolution (CDR) were not formed until twenty-one months after the fall of Batista, and even then their tasks were largely limited to vigilance against counterrevolutionaries. They have never taken on the scope that the CDSs have already achieved.
- The FSLN has already organized its own current in the trade-union movement, which has rapidly achieved predominance among Nicaraguan workers. The July 26 Movement did not seek a direct role in the Cuban unions until five months after January 1, 1959, and even then did not decisively counterpose its policies to those of the Stalinists and other reformist union officials and struggle to wrest leadership from them, as has happened in Nicaragua. It should also be noted here that the Cuban Stalinist party had a considerably stronger base in the urban proletariat than that of the three small pro-Moscow factions in Nicaragua today.
- A revolutionary army has been built at breakneck speed in Nicaragua, considerably faster than the Cuban one. In fact, ten months after their victory the Fidelistas faced a split in their army when the officers of an entire province went over to the counterrevolution.
- Militia units separate from the FSLN army emerged during the insurrection, and the FSLN now projects massively expanding them on a workplace and school basis. The Cubans initiated militias only ten months after coming to power and did not provide them with serious and extensive military training until the Bay of Pigs invasion of April 1961.
- While the Cubans permitted elements from Batista's police to remain in the new force they set up, the Sandinista National Police has been built entirely from revolutionary fighters.
- While the Cubans waited more than six months before resolutely building an intelligence service, the FSLN did so right away. At first the Cuban government even put an ex-Batistiano in charge of theirs.
- The land reform in Cuba was not launched until five months after the anti-Batista victory, while Nicaragua's INRA was set up immediately and now administers 30% of productive land and 60% of the big haciendas.
- Almost no corporations were nationalized in Cuba until August 1960. Nicaragua, in contrast, has already nationalized an important part of industry and commerce, all domestic-owned banks and insurance companies, and the imperialist-owned mines.
- In Cuba, with the exception of the temporary revolutionary tribunals that tried Batista's hangmen, the bourgeoisie controlled the entire court system and attempted to use it to block radical measures such as the land reform. The Cuban courts underwent an initial purge ten months after the revolutionary victory and then had to be purged again in 1960. The Nicaraguans have in practice suspended any fundamental role for the old court system.
- Finally, a key contrast is that between the political consciousness of the Castro team at the beginning and that of the current FSLN leadership. Castro claimed to be against communism in 1959; he counterposed "huma-

nism." He made no call for the formation of a revolutionary party, nor did he see the revolution as being inevitably a socialist one. Joseph Hansen pointed to the lack of socialist consciousness in Cuba in the 1959-60 period as one of the weaknesses in the Cuban process. In Nicaragua, it is clear that the central leaders and most of the experienced cadres of the FSLN consider themselves Marxists, view their organizations as the forerunner of a vanguard party, and see the revolution as necessarily a socialist one.

More examples could be cited. All indicate a more rapid tempo in Nicaragua and a more advanced consciousness on the part of both the leadership and the masses—not because the Sandinistas are more talented or determined than their Cuban counterparts were, but, in part, because the Nicaraguans have learned a great deal from their Cuban teachers. They have the Cuban example to study and stand on and have absorbed many lessons from that experience.

Weakened Imperialists Seek Openings

There is one other very important difference between the Cuban and Nicaraguan revolutions that we should note carefully—the relative world strength of U.S. imperialism.

The Cuban Revolution came before the Vietnam War of 1963-75. Nicaragua comes afterwards. In Cuba, the United States rulers underestimated the class dynamics of what they were up against, as well as the revolutionary qualities of the Fidelista leadership. The traditional methods of economic pressure and corruption were applied, ones that had been effective in the past in calling to order Latin American governments that threatened to get out of hand. These failed. Naturally, the U.S. imperialists decided never to make the same miscalculations again—as was revealed dramatically in Santo Domingo in 1965. They sent in tens of thousands of marines at the first sign of trouble.

The Vietnam War profoundly weakened U.S. imperialism, however. The most important aspect of this—probably the one least understood, including in Nicaragua today—was the change in the political consciousness of the masses of the American people. Opposition to Washington's foreign military interventions, and deep skepticism about the truth of any justifications emanating from the White House, became the hallmarks of the "Vietnam Syndrome."

Despite all efforts, Washington has not succeeded in reversing these deep-seated attitudes and increasing its flexibility in confronting the insurgent colonial masses.

This change in the class relationship of forces within the United States, and therefore the overall relationship of forces on an international scale, gave a boost to all anti-imperialist struggles. Cuba has been able to respond favorably to requests for military support from governments in Africa, for example, without Washington daring to counter this with its own troops.

The relative weakening of U.S. imperialism has had an impact on the bourgeoisie of the semicolonial countries as well.

In June 1979, U.S. pressure failed to get the Organization of American States to sanction an invasion of Nicaragua. When Washington probed the possibility of moving U.S. troops into the situation by landing helicopters and a communications unit in Costa Rica just prior to the Sandinista victory—with the excuse that they would help evacuate U.S. citizens—the result was a rapid repudiation by Costa Rica's bourgeois parliament, which was looking out for its own well-being in face of mass opposition from workers and students.

All this should not lead us to the illusion that the imperialists cannot sometimes partially reverse the present opposition to imperialist wars among the American people. They are working day and night to change this situation. Nor can we rule out that they might make military moves in defiance of public opinion. But the political limits on their use of military power have remained fundamentally unchanged since Vietnam—despite hostages in Iran, Afghan guerrillas, Soviet-brigade-in-Cuba scares, or Vietnamese boat people propaganda. Each advance of the world revolution helps to weaken the hold of chauvinist and racist ideas in the American working class.

We know that Washington aided Somoza militarily down to the last minute. While maneuvering with the FSLN in negotiations just prior to Somoza's fall, Washington did everything it could to try and save the National Guard from military defeat. Writing in the September-October issue of *New Left Review,* Harald Jung cites information leaked by the Panamanian secret police that lists the arms being flown to Somoza as late as July 6 from U.S. bases in Panama. U.S. arms were also sent in through El Salvador and Guatemala, while the Spanish imperialists helped out with military aid sent through Portugal and Guatemala. Better known are Israel's shipments to Somoza, obviously done in total collaboration with the White House. As Somoza was on his last legs, Edward Kennedy was calling for "any means, including military" to be used to prevent "the establishment of a Marxist regime" in Nicaragua. But they could not use massive U.S. military power to block the Sandinista victory.

There is no doubt that Washington is now desperately trying to shore up the bourgeois forces in Nicaragua. It is trying to maneuver within the existing international relationship of forces and is looking for any weak point in the Sandinistas' armour. We can be certain that the Pentagon is not making empty gestures with its military maneuvers in the Caribbean. The imperialists are looking for an opportunity to bring direct military pressures to bear against the Nicaraguan revolution.

But their options are limited.

If they are unable to prevent the creation of a second workers' state in the western hemisphere it will not be because of stupid policies, inattention, or a failure to draw the lessons of Cuba and Santo Domingo. It will be due to the relative weakening of U.S. imperialism *and* the revolutionary caliber of the Sandinista and Cuban leaderships.

In this regard, it's worth looking at the question of U.S. aid to Nicaragua.

In his interesting and informative article on workers' and farmers' governments, [*Workers and Farmers Governments Since the Second World War,* Education for Socialists Bulletin] Bob Chester posed the question of what might have happened in Cuba if Washington had followed the approach used by the French imperialists to block the formation of a workers' state in Algeria.

After watching the U.S. fiasco in Cuba and its own fiasco in Vietnam, Paris maneuvered differently in Algeria. The French rulers sought and attained a negotiated settlement before they could be dealt a total military defeat. They then posed as "friends" of the new Algeria, trying to ride out the ensuing mass upsurge. They offered aid to bolster the more conservative elements of the anti-French forces. In the first three years of the revolution, 23,000 French teachers and technicians were sent to Algeria. Loans amounting to some 800 million dollars were extended. In the end, given the deep contradictions in Algeria and political weakness of the leadership, French imperialism succeeded in halting the Algerian process half way, overturning the workers' and farmers' government, and reconsolidating a bourgeois state with its friends in power.

Is Washington attempting to follow a similar policy in Nicaragua today? They did not immediately launch an all-out frontal assault, politically, economically or militarily. They encouraged their Latin American allies to try to restrain the FSLN. They sent their social democratic lapdogs to Managua to offer aid as true socialists. They even invited leaders of the FSLN to Washington.

But as Congressional procrastination over a piddling $75 million in *loans* to Nicaragua indicates, Washington's course is not the same as the French imperialist strategy in Algeria. There are no investments, food shipments, medical aid or any other forms of economic assistance flooding into Nicaragua to try to buy off the revolution.

Is this pigheadedness or lack of intelligence on the part of Wall Street? Not understanding the more sophisticated European methods? I don't think so. Washington's assessment is clearly that the revolutionary upsurge of the masses has gone too deep, and the FSLN leadership is too resolute in carrying through its social measures in the interests of the workers and peasants of Nicaragua.

The French imperialist strategy toward the Algerian regime of Ben Bella is not a viable alternative. Why throw good money after bad?

The Coming Showdown

The FSLN has been maneuvering to gain time so as to achieve a few immediate and pressing goals—to build an army; to reactivate the economy and normalize production, seeking international aid as part of this; to initiate social reforms, organize the masses and raise their consciousness; and to stave off an imperialist invasion or blockade.

The FSLN's policy of giving concessions to sectors of the bourgeoisie in order to gain time has been correct. They have permitted capitalists to continue to function in exchange for their relaunching production. We should recall here that the Bolsheviks waited some eight months before even beginning to carry out any extensive nationalizations of industry. And even then they felt that circumstances had forced them to act faster than they would have preferred. Unfortunately this is usually the case—it is impossible to control all the factors that determine when nationalizations must be carried out. These involve political as well as economic reasons: it was the opening of the civil war that forced the Bolsheviks to act rapidly.

The Sandinistas are succeeding by and large in their effort to gain time. They have carried through their policies in the interests of the workers and peasants and have defended their course with skill. For instance, they did not openly abolish the Council of State but instead have called for one that is even more democratic. They have taken advantage of the widespread popularity they gained through the anti-Somoza struggle to get aid from Latin American bourgeois regimes, as well as to make it more difficult for the imperialists to mount a propaganda offensive against them. They ruled out immediate execution of Somoza's butchers, requested aid from the United States, offered concessions to sectors of the bourgeoisie in Nicaragua, and retained in their posts bourgeois figures who were already committed to participate in the new government prior to the fall of Somoza. Thus they turn the contradiction on the bourgeoisie—either go along with the pro-worker, pro-peasant course of the government or else be exposed before the masses.

It is rather telling that during the last six months this bourgeoisie has only been able to form tiny splinter political formations and has no political arm with any mass base. The bourgeois parties have not been able to hold a single political meeting addressed to the workers and peasants or organized in a plebian neighborhood.

As we have explained, the great contradiction in Nicaragua today is that the pro-worker, pro-peasant measures and the mobilization, organization, and education of the masses run directly counter to the preservation of a capitalist economy. If any illusions have arisen that it is possible to permit major capitalist holdings indefinitely parallel to the development of an economy planned in the interests of the toiling masses, reality will rapidly dissipate them.

Nicaragua is now entering a new period. It is no longer a question of simply opening factories and warehouses. Investment and growth of the economy must take place. It will go forward on a capitalist foundation or on the basis of nationalization and economic planning. The revolutionary army is rapidly being consolidated; the masses are more organized each day. There will be no major new breakthroughs in aid, since the imperialists and the national bourgeoisies of Latin America can see as clearly as we do that the FSLN will not turn over governmental power to the bourgeoisie and is refusing therefore to reconsolidate a capitalist state.

The national bourgeoisie inside Nicaragua has been divided over what to do. Many have chosen to vote with their feet and get out. For others this is not so easy: if your capital is in land, you cannot take it with you. This is the situation of a great part of the national bourgeoisie. Whatever capital can be removed is being removed—of Nicaragua's estimated 2 million head of cattle, 300,000 have been driven out of the country illegally into Honduras or Costa Rica.

Other bourgeois families have chosen to stay and fight it out. This position is reflected in the editorial line of the daily *La Prensa,* the main rallying point of the bourgeoisie in Nicaragua. Not having any political party of any standing (the two traditional bourgeois parties, the Liberals and Conservatives, collapsed with the anti-Somoza victory), the bourgeoisie is forced to act politically through its economic organizations (the Chamber of Commerce, Chamber of Industry, and so on). On November 14 these groups submitted a united political statement of their demands. In short, they called for a bourgeois government, a bourgeois army and police, and a policy of labor discipline. Without these, they said, they could have no "confidence." This is the bourgeois way of saying, "We will not invest." Without investment, production stops.

The workers have begun protesting attempts by the Nicaraguan capitalists to disinvest. The union at Managua's big Sears department store, for example, alerted the government in mid-December that the management there was sending capital and goods out of the country. Similar reports come from other parts of the country.

Nicaragua faces a difficult situation between now and May. This is the dry season. Crops are not planted in this period. Do not forget that Nicaragua is an overwhelmingly agricultural country. Many rural workers normally find employment picking cotton in this period, but since the civil war hit at planting time last year, only a small percentage of the normal cotton crop was sown.

Emergency measures will have to be taken during this period to feed the population and create jobs. This will be difficult. As the next planting season begins, INRA officials have made it clear, capitalist landowners who do not plant will face expropriation. Factories that do not produce will also be subject to expropriation. And each expropriation will only lead to still less confidence—and growing desperation—among the remaining bourgeoisie.

The exact tempo of this coming confrontation cannot be predicted. What we can be sure of, though, is that this showdown is coming and that it will either open the way for the creation of the second workers' state in the Americas—a victory for the working class that would have enormous ramifications—or else it will place the present advances of the workers and peasants in Nicaragua in jeopardy.

Workers' Democracy

A great deal of workers' democracy exists in Nicaragua today. National congresses of the mass organizations have been held or are being planned. Preparations for electing representatives from these organizations to a new Council of State are opening up rather promising perspectives for a further expansion of workers' democracy.

The FSLN does not have a clear programmatic position on workers' democracy. Its error of labeling the ultraleft sectarians as Somozaist counterrevolutionaries has been partially corrected. But this correction in practice has not been accompanied by any codification of a policy of workers' democracy. It is not clearly seen as a class question.

For example, the FSLN's current policy of allowing the largest ultraleft current in the workers' movement to publish their daily paper, *El Pueblo,* is seen as equivalent to permitting the bourgeoisie to bring out *La Prensa.* Likewise, the legal existence of political parties coming out of the workers' movement, such as the ultraleft People's Action Movement and the various reformist pro-Moscow factions, is associated with permitting the small bourgeois parties to function openly.

No organization coming out of the Fidelista current in Latin America has ever developed a clear understanding that it is in the interest of the revolution, of the working class, to permit the broadest possible discussion and democratic rights within the workers' movement and that this is not in contradiction to suppressing the special prerogatives and advantages of the bourgeoisie when necessary. This is an important difference between the Sandinistas' program and the views of Leninism. The Sandinistas are not familiar with, or do not understand, how it was that Lenin could build a party in which the right to form tendencies and factions was respected, where debates raged continually over policy, and where Lenin himself was sometimes voted down, while at the same time maintaining iron unity and discipline, leading a civil war, defeating a host of invading imperialist armies, and so on.

Fidelista currents often split when political differences arise, because they have no internal democratic forms to work out such disagreements. That is what happened to the FSLN. It split into three currents when its leaders became divided over how best to carry out the struggle to overthrow Somoza. Fortunately the FSLN, with Cuban help, overcame this division. And they might draw some important lessons from this experience.

We should at the same time note what the FSLN has already learned from some negative experiences with the Stalinists. The FSLN leadership is capable of learning rapidly from its own experiences, considers Lenin to have been a great revolutionist, and is open to learning from the Russian example.

The FSLN leadership is a highly experienced group, politically knowledgeable, and not monolithic (except against the enemies of the revolution). Joe Hansen wrote in one of his articles that "the next revolutionary victory, wherever it comes, will in all likelihood go even further than the Cuban Revolution in departing from the deformation imposed by the pernicious heritage of Stalinism." Nicaragua may prove him correct. It is certainly true so far. The empirical experience with the workers' democracy that has already developed and its value in strengthening the revolution may affect in a positive manner the thinking of the Nicaraguan revolutionary leadership.

The FSLN and Trotskyism

There have been occasional reports of attacks on Trotskyism by FSLN leaders. Recently, right here in New York, Commander Víctor Tirado of the FSLN National Directorate—when egged on by a questioner from one of the sectarian outfits—referred to Trotskyism in derogatory terms at a news conference.

Since its founding in 1962, the FSLN has only had minor contact with the Fourth International, which for many years did not have a single organization anywhere in Central America.

Certain contacts were established with Sandinistas in exile in Europe and in Mexico, especially in the late 1960s and early 1970s. Some FSLN cadres became aware of the fact that there are differing currents that all use the name of Trotskyism.

As the FSLN came to power in July, it was suddenly confronted with several groups inside Nicaragua calling themselves Trotskyist. Some of them were, at the time, members of the Fourth International; all were acting in a totally sectarian, provocative manner.

First there was the notorious Simón Bolívar Brigade adventure launched by Nahuel Moreno, which we are all too familiar with. Moreno, well known as a Latin American Trotskyist, set out to build up his own little power base in Nicaragua, falsely using the name of the FSLN to raise material support and win positions among the masses. Moreno saw the FSLN as the central problem in Nicaragua and incredibly enough set out to take leadership away from them! The motivation for all this was Moreno's factional operation within the Fourth International. To the FSLN, Moreno's actions understandably seemed incomprehensible. Who would ever consider sending fifty or more cadres to disrupt the Nicaraguan revolution at the moment of its victory? Knowing little about the Fourth International, about Moreno, or about the internal faction fight in the Fourth International, the FSLN's suspicion was that the CIA was probably behind the whole affair. It seemed unbelievable that anyone on the left would carry out the kind of provocative acts the Morenistas did.

Secondly, we have Fausto Amador's Socialist Workers Organization (OST) in Costa Rica. The OST was well known to the FSLN since many of them had been active in Costa Rica and because Fausto, the brother of FSLN founder Carlos Fonseca, was notorious for his break with the FSLN in 1969.

The problem in relation to Fausto Amador, however, is not the mistakes he made when he split from the FSLN. Those he publicly acknowledged before he joined the Fourth International. The political errors proved to be much deeper. As one can see by rereading articles by him—which like many other articles that appear in the pages of *Intercontinental Press,* were published for the information of the Fourth International—his sectarianism toward the FSLN leadership made him incapable of accurately assessing the objective situation in Nicaragua. He didn't think the FSLN could succeed in ousting Somoza and when they did, he proved too subjective to recognize the revolutionary victory and what it *proved* about the Sandinista—and Fidelista—leaderships.

The OST continues to hold that the FSLN leadership is today the primary obstacle to the advance of the Nicaraguan revolution. Like Moreno they have set out to replace the Sandinistas with themselves as the only truly revolutionary leadership!

Finally, there was in Nicaragua a small, sectarian group called the Revolutionary Marxist League (LMR). It had appeared in the mid-1970s and asked for membership in the Fourth International, and presented itself in Nicaragua as an affiliate of the International. It too had and has a very sectarian line toward the FSLN and the revolution.

After all this it would not be at all surprising if FSLN leaders gave credence to the anti-Trotskyist slanders they often hear from Stalinists, or at best considered Trotskyists to be hopeless sectarians.

In fact, the Sandinistas are not well acquainted with the program, history, or activities of the world Trotskyist movement, the Fourth International. They are suspicious after the experiences they have gone through, although they are also becoming more and more aware that there are sharp differences among groups that call themselves Trotskyist and that some of these groups, in fact the majority, are not sectarians and are defending the Nicaraguan revolution.

The fact that most of the worst sectarian forces have now gathered together under one roof—the so-called Parity Committee set up by Moreno's Bolshevik Faction, the predominantly French Leninist-Trotskyist Tendency, the Costa Rican OST and Lambert's Organizing Committee for the Reconstruction of the Fourth International—helps clear up the picture.

The sectarian groups—what Tomás Borge calls the "idiots"—are not agents of imperialism. They do echo inside the workers' movement counterrevolutionary propaganda against the Nicaraguan revolution, as a by-product of their ultraleft sectarian politics. No other left current in the world of any standing has attempted to hold public meetings attacking the revolutionary government of Nicaragua except these sectarians. In France, Mexico, Brazil, Canada, Britain and possibly elsewhere they have actually held meetings to condemn so-called repression against workers and leftists in Nicaragua. Such acts have a counterrevolutionary content. They show the depth of degeneration of these organizations. Revolutions, like wars, can suddenly bring to the surface processes that have been gestating in organizations for a long time. The Nicaraguan revolution brought out a deep sectarian sickness among some organizations calling themselves Trotskyist. The Fourth International was too healthy an organism to succumb to the illness and as things became clarified this rapidly led to a split.

Despite the fact that the Fourth International has parted ways with those incapable of recognizing a revolution when it happens, there are still indications of sectarian pressures within the Fourth International. One example was the majority position in the United Secretariat, which, while correctly criticizing the Simón Bolívar Brigade in sharp clear terms, nonetheless insisted on criticizing the FSLN as well for expelling the brigade from Nicaragua. The SWP Political Committee has stated publicly that we are not in a position to judge what tactics the FSLN had to use to stop the adventurist and criminal activity of the Simón Bolívar Brigade. We recognize the right of the FSLN to act, and we do not agree with the criticisms adopted by the majority of the United Secretariat.

The FSLN leaders are not sectarians. They want aid from all groups and political currents that are willing to defend the revolution. More than that, they indicate their desire to have relations, to have a dialogue with all revolutionists.

As I have said, the Sandinista leaders begin from a position of general suspicion about all forces associated with Trotskyism. But they are independent-minded and revolutionary. They inevitably feel a certain attraction for forces like themselves that are also revolutionists. They will judge others by how they apply their ideas, not simply by their claims to be revolutionary, proletarian internationalists or firm partisans of the Transitional Program.

When we began our extensive coverage of Nicaragua in *Perspectiva Mundial* we decided to send some copies to Nicaragua so that revolutionists there would be correctly informed of our positions. The interest in *PM* there has been quite exciting. In fact, many readers have actually been perplexed at seeing a magazine that defends revolutionary positions with which they fully agree while learning that *PM* is put out by Trotskyists, who they had thought were counterrevolutionaries or sectarians!

The FSLN leaders are aware of and appreciate the efforts of the Socialist Workers Party to get information out about the Nicaraguan revolution and participate in the solidarity movement. This means exactly that—no more and no less. As the struggle deepens in Nicaragua and American imperialism begins to play even rougher, they will judge us by what we do.

Tasks of Fourth International

At its World Congress in November, the Fourth International voted to make solidarity with the Nicaraguan revolution its central international campaign. We carry out this work in a nonsectarian manner. For the Socialist Workers Party this work is even more important because we are inside the United States; it is our own country's government that is the main counterrevolutionary force the Nicaraguan revolution must confront.

There have been various tactical problems involved in getting this work off the ground—a combination of objective factors, such as the near blackout of news on Nicaragua in the bourgeois press and the fake stand of sympathy by the U.S. government, and the subjective factors related to the political weaknesses of the workers' movement in the United States. But the SWP has been exemplary in providing factual information on Nicaragua to help educate political forces within the United States as well as in other countries. We have begun to devote a considerable amount of energy to the solidarity campaign and we should now step this up.

Sections of the Fourth International in many parts of the world are also campaigning strongly in defense of Nicaragua. Some that could be mentioned are the Mexican Revolutionary Workers Party (PRT), which has organized days of solidarity in which their entire organization has taken to the streets, in collaboration with FSLN representatives, to raise money for Nicaragua. Or we could point to the examplary participation of the Colombian Revolutionary Socialist Party (PSR) in that country's united-front solidarity committee. In Europe, the comrades of the French Revolutionary Communist League (LCR) sponsored a meeting of 2,500 in Paris to kick off their effort of solidarity, and in many other countries, such as Spain, Britain, Canada, and the Netherlands, our comrades are involved. The Australian and New Zealand comrades have made the decision to get deeply involved.

We must recognize at this plenum that 1980 will be a critical year in Nicaragua. We are bound to see some rapid shifts in imperialist policy that will entail important responsibilities—and opportunities—for our movement. We must act now so as to be in a position to move as events develop.

The imperialists will not sit back and permit another workers' state to appear in Latin America without a fight. The U.S. government will go all out—using every possible method, every dirty trick in the CIA manual, every criminal act, from sabotage to assassination attempts against FSLN leaders to military force—to try and block the consolidation of the victory of the Nicaraguan proletariat. There is no way to predict just what forms this will take. We must be prepared for the possibility that they will act, up to and including the use of military intervention. We must prepare, just as the Nicaraguans are preparing, for any eventuality. By doing our part here, as we did during the Vietnam War, we can be an important factor in the equation that will decide the battle.

We know the Cuban leadership and the Nicaraguan leadership have shown themselves to be capable politicians in making it as difficult as possible for imperialism to mount an open military intervention. They have correctly combined military preparations with a political offensive aimed at building international solidarity and limiting the imperialists' options.

The FSLN has taken a deep and direct interest in developing international solidarity work, and has taken a nonsectarian approach in their relations with all organizations involved in this work.

The rising radicalization in Central America, not only in El Salvador but also in Guatemala, Honduras, Costa Rica, and Panama adds another favorable factor in the defense of the Nicaraguan revolution.

We hold that the world situation is favorable for a victory in Nicaragua.

To sum up, the resolution before us outlines the unfolding process of permanent revolution in Nicaragua. Beginning with a struggle to bring down a brutal dictatorship, and establish their right to self-determination, the workers and peasants are being driven by necessity to oppose capitalism. When Trotsky first noted that in the epoch of imperialism it is impossible for the colonial and semicolonial countries, under capitalism, to win their full freedom and break out of the backwardness imperialism has imposed upon them, no one had seen the list of examples—Yugoslavia, Vietnam, China, Cuba—that we now have behind us. Today, it is more clear than ever in a case like Nicaragua that a bourgeois revolution that would create a new advanced capitalist country is ruled out historically. Only the Cuban road, the road of socialist revolution, permits accomplishing the bourgeois-democratic tasks—land reform, independence, democratic rights, and economic development.

Whether the Nicaraguan leaders recognize this as Trotsky's theory of the permanent revolution or as the lessons of the Cuban revolution, or simply come to this conclusion empirically out of their own experiences, it is an essential acquisition for a correct strategy in the coming period.

The resolution holds that the formation of a workers' state will be posed in the coming months, owing to the contradiction between the gains and victories of the revolution thus far and the continued existence of capitalism in Nicaragua. The resolution will arm us with a correct approach to the FSLN, which we see as the beginning of a mass revolutionary party in Nicaragua, and toward the government, a workers' and farmers' government.

Our efforts here, as well as those of our comrades in other countries, can become an important factor in consolidating the proletarian victory in Nicaragua. This in turn can open up fresh possibilities to move forward to overcoming the most pressing need of the world proletariat, the building of a mass proletarian and revolutionary international to provide leadership in the world class struggle.

Despite the differences that do exist, primarily because of the different historical origins of the Sandinista National Liberation Front and the Fourth International, as we see it there are no differences between us that should block our being in the same revolutionary international. For many reasons this is not easily achievable, certainly not in the short run. But it is an indication of the correctness and timeliness of Trotsky's advice to be on the lookout for the appearance of "revolutionists of action" who emerge from their own particular experiences—in part because of the weakness of the Fourth International itself—and to recognize in these revolutionists an extremely important contingent for the building of the world party of socialist revolution.

Revolution in Nicaragua

[The general line of the following resolution was adopted by the Socialist Workers Party National Committee January 5, 1980.]

* * *

The primary purpose of the following theses is to clarify (1) the class character of the Nicaraguan government today, and (2) why the Nicaraguan revolution and the evolution of the Sandinista National Liberation Front are central to our strategic task of building the world party of socialist revolution necessary to lead the toilers in the overthrow of world capitalism.

* * *

1. Between late May and July 19, 1979, deepgoing popular insurrections in the main cities of Nicaragua—prepared by the Sandinista National Liberation Front (FSLN) and coordinated with an FSLN military offensive—toppled the United States-backed dictatorship of Anastasio Somoza. The victory was the culmination of two months of general strikes and armed uprisings in the cities by the workers, semiproletarian masses, youth, and sectors of the petty bourgeoisie; land occupations and other mobilizations by the poor peasants and agricultural laborers in the rural districts; and stepped-up guerrilla operations and a concerted military drive by the FSLN.

These were the motor forces of the climactic stage in the struggle against the dictatorship and U.S. imperialism. They gave the revolution a powerful anticapitalist impulse.

The final year of the revolutionary struggle was marked by widespread organization of the masses in neighborhood committees and self-defense units, as well as by increased organization in workplaces and the countryside. This occurred both on the initiative of the FSLN and spontaneously in response to the worsening living conditions and brutal repression under Somoza. In addition, as the final struggle gathered momentum the ranks of the FSLN's military units were swelled by thousands of young workers, poor peasants, students, the unemployed, and radicalized petty-bourgeois forces. This included many Latin Americans from other countries who joined the fight against Somozaism and Yankee imperialism.

As one city after another was liberated from Somoza's National Guard under the combined blows of FSLN units and popular insurrections, Civil Defense Committees (CDC) and militias organized military defense and took over such vital tasks in the neighborhoods as food distribution, health care, sanitation, and the dispensation of justice to Somozaist torturers. Sandinista Workers Defense Committees (CDTS) arose in some factories and workplaces, the nuclei of what was to become the Sandinista Workers Federation (CST). Other mass organizations—the women's group AMPRONAC (later to become the Association of Nicaraguan Women), the Rural Workers Association (ATC), the July 19 Sandinista Youth, the teachers union (ANDEN)—also got their start in the period before and during the insurrection.

Alongside this intervention of the toiling masses and development of proletarian forms of organization, the bourgeois forces opposed to Somoza underwent a process of disintegration. Most desperately sought a compromise with the dictatorship while some belatedly threw in their lot with the insurrection. This sharp shift in the relationship of class forces is a key factor in explaining the dynamics of the socialist revolution now unfolding in Nicaragua.

Triumph Over Somoza

2. Following Somoza's flight on July 17, the disintegration of the National Guard accelerated. His stand-in Francisco Urcuyo had promised to transfer power to a five-person junta of the Government of National Reconstruction (GRN). This was supposed to pave the way for the integration of some National Guard units into the new army and the appointment of a bourgeois-dominated Council of State. The formation of this junta and its responsibilities had been announced July 9 in Costa Rica as part of the post-Somoza governmental program agreed to by the FSLN and some of the bourgeois opposition forces.

With United States support, however, Urcuyo attempted to hold on to state power, and demanded the FSLN lay down its arms. This provoked the final FSLN push on Managua and a popular mass uprising there in which Somoza's "bunker" was captured and tens of thousands of weapons were seized and distributed. The GRN program had stated that the new army would incorporate "soldiers and officers who demonstrated honest and patriotic conduct" and were not guilty of "corruption, repression, [and] crimes against the people." But the section of Somoza's National Guard that did not escape to Honduras scattered under the impact of the mass insurrection.

The revolutionary triumph over Somocismo was thus a sweeping one, in which large sections of the previous state apparatus—in particular the entire repressive apparatus—were dismantled and replaced, resolving the situation of dual power that had developed in Nicaragua in the final weeks prior to Somoza's fall. As a result, the effort to establish a well-trained professional Sandinista army is being entirely built around a cadre of FSLN guerrillas and militia fighters.

The triumph in Managua, following that in other main cities, achieved with organized mass participation and by revolutionary means, established both the FSLN's leadership authority among the masses and its decisive political decision-making power. The contrast during the drive to victory between the courage and dedication of the Sandinistas and the hesitations and maneuvers of the bourgeois opposition did not go unnoticed in the working-class neighborhoods or in the countryside. It had a profound impact on the consciousness of FSLN militants and leaders, and on the political course they have followed.

3. It soon became obvious that the new governing power—the way in which important decisions of state were actually being made and implemented—was qualitatively different from the bourgeois coalition government projected in the July 9 GRN program and the Fundamental Statute decreed July 20.

The five-person junta that replaced Somoza took the form of a coalition of three FSLN leaders with two figures from the bourgeois opposition. This was similar to the form taken by the junta's cabinet of ministers: several of the initial appointees were FSLN leaders (e.g., Interior, Agrarian Reform, and Social Welfare), while others—including the head of the Central Bank—were bourgeois figures, usually serving alongside FSLN vice-ministers.

But this is not the totality of the actual government. In fact, the key elements of the new state structure fall outside the framework promised in the July 9 program of the GRN.

The government itself includes the FSLN leadership, the Sandinista armed forces, as well as INRA (Nicaraguan Institute of Agrarian Reform) and to some extent the mass organizations led by the FSLN.

The GRN program stipulated the appointment of a Council of State. This body was to "share legislative powers" with the junta, draw up drafts of a new constitution and electoral law, appoint the judiciary, and have the power to veto, with a two-thirds vote, decisions taken by the junta.

By agreement prior to the Managua insurrection, the Council of State was to be composed of thirty-three representatives from the bourgeois opposition parties, the chambers of commerce and industry and other capitalist organs, the Catholic Church hierarchy, the FSLN, trade unions, and other groups. Its proposed composition guaranteed bourgeois domination. For its part the FSLN was to have had somewhere in the range of six members. The Nicaraguan capitalists and imperialism counted on the council to serve as a brake on the social and economic measures instituted following Somoza's downfall and to be the institution that exercises sovereignty. It was to draft a bourgeois constitution according to which a bourgeois judicial system, headed by a Supreme Court, would block "unconstitutional" inroads on property and other "normal" bourgeois prerogatives.

In the first weeks following July 19, it was widely assumed that the Council of State would be rapidly installed. A tentative convocation date of September 15 was even announced. But that date came and went, and amid growing agitation by bourgeois forces for the convocation of the Council of State, the junta announced October 22 that convocation of the council was being postponed until May 4, 1980. In the intervening months it was to be "restructured" to provide representation above all to the new mass organizations—the CDSs, CST, ATC, women's association, Sandinista youth, etc. These organizations, with FSLN backing, have launched a campaign demanding the Council of State be a council of toilers dominated by CDS representation and that of other mass organizations.

The postponement and proposed restructuring of the Council of State represents one of the major results on the governmental level so far of the dramatic shift in the relationship of class forces as the revolutionary process has deepened in Nicaragua.

Nothing has been done to begin drafting a bourgeois constitution to provide legitimacy to capitalist rule. Instead, in late August the junta decreed a "Statute on the Rights of Nicaraguans" that not only guarantees basic political freedoms such as speech, press, and assembly, but also women's equality and the priority of the social and economic rights of the toilers over the property and prerogatives of the capitalists.

Furthermore, the entire judicial system was purged, and while a Supreme Court has been appointed, as described in the GRN program, its functions are limited to matters such as divorce cases.

In addition, some ministries initially headed by bourgeois figures had no fundamental decision-making authority. The most striking example of this was the Ministry of Defense, nominally headed by ex-National Guard Col. Bernardino Larios (who led a coup attempt against Somoza in 1978 and later fled to Panama). Larios had no authority whatsoever over the Sandinista People's Army (EPS), which since its formation has been firmly under the command of the Sandinista Front. The commander-in-chief of the EPS, FSLN leader Humberto Ortega, was named not by Larios or even by the GRN junta, but rather by the FSLN Joint National Directorate. (The decision was later ratified by the junta.)

In late December, Larios was replaced by Humberto Ortega as part of a broad governmental reorganization. (Ortega remains commander-in-chief.) Not once during his brief term in office did Larios issue a statement, hold a news conference, or appear at a public event.

The reorganized Ministry of Defense will oversee all the Sandinista armed forces. The Sandinista People's Militias are to be greatly expanded, under the direction of newly named Vice-Minister of Defense Edén Pastora ("Commander Zero"). The Sandinista National Police, constructed from the bottom up out of young Sandinista fighters, fall under the Ministry of the Interior, headed by FSLN Comandante Tomás Borge.

The Ministry of Planning was initially headed by bourgeois technocrat Roberto Mayorga. He has now been displaced by FSLN Comandante Henry Ruiz, who explained upon taking the post that the planning ministry "is the key to the present situation, and the FSLN National Directorate has thought it necessary to assign a member of the Directorate to this post." Ruiz will oversee implementation of the 1980 Plan for Economic Reactivation, which represents the new government's initial steps toward economic planning.

In the field of agriculture, all major decisions and policy statements have been made and implemented by the Nicaraguan Institute of Agrarian Reform (INRA), headed by FSLN Comandante Jaime Wheelock. Modeled after Cuba's INRA, this agency was not mentioned in the GRN's July 9 program or the Fundamental Statute.

INRA, which has branches in every province of the country, was consolidated at the end of December under the revamped Ministry of Agricultural Development, which Wheelock was appointed to head (retaining the post of INRA director). The first minister of agricultural development, a landowner appointed in July, had been in a similar position to that of defense minister Larios.

The FSLN's National Directorate functions as a source and wielder of governing power outside the terms of the GRN accord. This was politically codified on September 1, 1979, when, during a military parade and rally to spur construction of the EPS, the nine members of the National Directorate were proclaimed "Comandantes de la Revolución," that is, of the entire process and not simply of the army or the formal government. During this initial stage of the revolution, it is the Comandantes of the Revolution—not the bourgeoisie operating through the Council of State as they had planned—who have played the decisive role governing together with the Sandinista-dominated junta.

The rising importance of new mass organizations and especially of the CDSs (none of which were contemplated in the GRN program) is among the most outstanding of the postliberation developments. It is on the expansion and consolidation of the CDSs, the unions of workers and peasants, the other mass organizations, and the Sandinista Army, that the authority of the FSLN is largely based. To varying degrees, all of these are already taking on decision-making and administrative functions at the workplace, farm, neighborhood, and muncipal levels. By the end of 1979, province-wide coordination of the CDSs was under way and one national gathering of CDS representatives had already been held. Sandinista leaders have announced that a delegated CDS congress will be held early in 1980.

So the government that was consolidated soon after Somoza's fall is not that projected by the GRN program.

Social and Economic Steps

4. The accumulation of progressive social and economic measures in the first months of the revolution demonstrates that the Nicaraguan toilers, under FSLN leadership, have set off down a promising road oriented toward expropriation of the bourgeoisie:

• The new government immediately nationalized the entire Somoza and Somozaist assets in agriculture, real estate, banking, industry, commerce, transport, fishing fleets, shipyard and port equipment, and communications media property.

• It nationalized all domestic banking and imposed strict controls on foreign banks. This is a necessary first step toward channeling resources, directing them to expanding such needs as education, housing, and hospitals, and initiating measures of economic planning.

• It launched an extensive agrarian reform on Somozaist land, bringing under state control some 60 percent of the big landholdings currently under cultivation. In collaboration with the ATC, INRA is transforming these haciendas into state farms on which the agricultural laborers will participate in administrative tasks. Peasant cooperatives are being encouraged on the smaller nationalized holdings, and some land redistribution has taken place in response to the demands of peasants with tiny plots. Debt foreclosure on the farms of small proprietors has been abolished.

• The government took control over all export trade of agricultural cash commodities such as cotton, coffee, sugar, beef, and fish. A state monopoly (ENABAS) has been established for the purchase and sale of all grains and agrichemical products. Similar state monopolies have been set up for the purchase and sale of all other major crops (coffee, cotton, sugar, etc.).

• While pledging to renegotiate and honor Nicaragua's legitimate foreign debt, the government immediately cancelled Somoza's arms debts to the Israeli and Argentine governments. It then announced it would study carefully all other debts contracted by the dictatorship to determine which ones were illegitmate—that is, had been arranged through corrupt dealings or had simply wound up in private Somocista bank accounts abroad. Meanwhile, given the virtually empty treasury left by Somoza, the new government has declared a de facto moratorium on interest and repayment.

• It nationalized the essential means of land, sea, and air transport. The television system and several of the radio networks have been expropriated and are being used by the FSLN to present its views to the population. The Sandinista daily *Barricada* is produced in the plant that previously printed the Somozaist newspaper, *Novedades*.

• It launched programs to reorganize and upgrade education, health care, social security, and other social services.

• The government issued a radical currency reform measure that—under the slogan "Let's take back from Somocismo the money that belongs to the people"—stopped Somozaists or other businessmen abroad from exchanging their cordobas for dollars held inside Nicaragua. All 500 and 1000 cordoba notes were withdrawn and investigations were begun into many large holdings. This measure helped slow the devaluation of the cordoba, and combat capitalist economic sabotage. Deposits under 3,000 cordobas were returned within a few days of the measure; at the end of October, following registration of the bank notes, the government began redeeming the certificates of deposit issued to holders of the notes inside Nicaragua.

• It has adopted an outspoken anti-imperialist stance on vital world political questions such as Indochina, the Mideast, southern Africa, and Carter's war moves against Cuba, the Caribbean, and Central America. The outpouring of more than 30,000 in Managua to greet Vietnamese Premier Pham Van Dong, one of the largest mass demonstrations since the revolutionary victory, was a big blow to the imperialist campaign to isolate Vietnam as an international pariah. U.S. imperialism was condemned for its aggression during the "Soviet brigade" crisis.

Following the October military coup in El Salvador, Moscow was quick to approve the new Washington-backed regime, signalling to the imperialists its willingness to help preserve capitalist stability in the area. The Nicaraguan government, along with the Cuban, refused to do so.

• The new government has continued its efforts to construct a centralized professional army to defend the revolutionary conquests against imperialism, the Somozaist forces and other class enemies both inside Nicaragua and beyond its borders.

• Having integrated most of the militia fighters into the EPS and Sandinista police, FSLN leaders have announced their intention to strengthen and reorganize a volunteer national militia on the basis of regular training in the workplace and in high schools and universities. Weapons are to be kept in the factories and controlled by the milicianos.

• After decades of tyrannical rule under which even the most elementary bourgeois-democratic liberties were ground into the dust, there has been an enormous expansion of democratic rights, including institutions of workers democracy, fostered by the new government. The CDSs and other popular bodies operate on the basis of democratic elections. The Bill of Rights guarantees not only basic freedoms such as speech, press, and assembly, but also the right to unionize and strike and to "organize political parties or groups, or to belong to them." The FSLN has strengthened the Sandinista-led CST trade-union federation in political competition with the old union federations led by the Stalinists, Christian Democrats and bourgeois business-unionists closely linked to the U.S. AFL-CIO bureaucracy. Workers have held democratic assemblies to choose their leaders and decide which federation to affiliate with; this has often resulted in unions previously part of one of the old federations joining the CST.

• The agrarian reform has also included "interventions" (that is, takeovers short of outright nationalization) of some lands owned by members of the bourgeois anti-Somoza opposition. Since there is a top priority on raising crops for food and vital foreign exchange, this most often targets landlords who refuse to cultivate their land.

• There have been further nationalizations and interventions; again including properties of "anti-Somozaist" capitalists. These have been carried out on the basis of economic need or because of illegitimate or antilabor operations by the owners. All insurance companies were nationalized in mid-October. This complements the nationalizations of the banks by giving the government further control over the flow of capital and lays the foundation for future economic planning.

• The FSLN is campaigning to organize peasants and rural laborers into the ATC and workers into the CST. In addition, the Sandinistas are taking steps to prepare and extend workers control over production in the nationalized sectors.

• At the beginning of November, the first major imperialist property was nationalized—the mines. (Domestic holdings in the mining sector were also taken over.) This further strengthens the government control over the country's natural resources and lays the basis for improving the wretched and extremely dangerous conditions under which Nicaragua's miners were forced to work.

• Sharp reductions in housing rents were decreed on December 19. Rents of less than $50 a month were cut by 50% and those of $50 to $100 a month were cut 60%. Rents over $100 a month were also substantially reduced under the new law, which also stipulates that the Ministry of Housing can reduce rents to below 50% of their old rates and can take over slum dwellings that have inadequate sanitary conditions.

• Housing reconstruction aid in the devastated popular neighborhoods has been initiated by the government. State control has been applied in housing developments built or operating in violation of real estate and tax laws. The first major public works projects have been initiated in this sector.

• A big increase in pensions and other social benefits to the aged and indigent has been decreed.

• Price controls have been established on basic food items. The government has authorized the CDSs to operate as price committees to enforce these controls, and the CDSs in the big open-air markets of Managua have taken the lead in this task.

• An enormous nationwide drive has been launched to wipe out illiteracy, a problem that is prevalent throughout Nicaragua but especially widespread among the rural population. All students above the sixth-grade level are to be mobilized in this "crusade for literacy"; and the country's schools are to be shut down for four months so that these students and all teachers can fully participate. Material, technical, and personnel aid is coming from Cuba for this campaign, which is being explicitly modeled on the way that country wiped out illiteracy in the early 1960s. As that experience showed, such a literacy drive is an important aid to firmly winning the poor peasantry to the side of the revolution, and defending it against counterrevolution.

Workers and Peasants Government

5. The FSLN-led government, based on Nicaragua's proletarian, semiproletarian, peasant, and radicalized petty-bourgeois masses, has initiated deep-going inroads against capitalist property in agriculture, industry, and finance. It has launched an ambitious program of social and cultural betterment for the Nicaraguan toilers. It has begun to construct a new armed power through the EPS and Sandinista police. Its radical policies have helped the FSLN spur the development of proletarian organizations through the CDSs, the trade unions, and other mass organizations. It has continued to foster mass mobilizations. The latest—a November 7 demonstration to honor FSLN founder Carlos Fonseca Amador—brought over 100,000 people into the streets of Managua. It was the largest outpouring since Somoza's fall.

The structures and direction of development established through all these measures indicate that this new regime has not only broken the armed might of the bourgeoisie. It has displaced the *political* power of the capitalists, taken decisive steps to block the establishment of a bourgeois government and refused to subordinate the interests of the exploited to the bourgeoisie's needs either nationally or internationally.

All this points to the conclusion that the Sandinista-led regime in Nicaragua is neither definitively bourgeois nor proletarian at this time. It is a *workers and peasants government*, of the kind described in the Transitional Program as "a government independent of the bourgeoisie" and at the Fourth Congress of the Communist International as a government that is "born out of the struggle of the masses, is supported by workers' bodies that are capable of fighting, bodies created by the most oppressed sections of the working masses."

By recognizing the new government in Nicaragua as a workers and peasants government, we signify:

a. its origin in an anti-dictatorial and anti-imperialist movement with a radical political program;

b. its coming to power as the result of a popular mass struggle, culminating in a civil war and tumultuous urban insurrections;

c. its resoluteness in combating and disarming the counterrevolution;

d. its tendency to respond by practical measures to popular demands for action against the urban and rural exploiters and against imperialism;

e. The capacity of its leading force, the FSLN, with whatever hesitations and political limitations, to undertake measures against bourgeois political and economic power and prerogatives. The exact stage in the development of these measures is not decisive in determining the class character of the regime; the decisive factor is the capacity and tendency of the leadership to move in this direction.

Combined with these factors is the FSLN's explicit identification of the revolutionary process in Nicaragua with the Cuban workers state, and with the anti-imperialist internationalism of the Castro leadership. Cuba's accomplishments under its social system are repeatedly held up as a model—in speeches, in *Barricada,* and over radio and television.

The Nicaraguan workers and peasants government, despite its many unique features, is similar to the regimes described by the Fourth International that arose and governed in Cuba from mid-1959 to late 1960 (when the expropriation of the bourgeoisie and the consolidation of the workers state was completed); and in Algeria from late 1963 to mid-1965 (when Boumedienne ousted Ben Bella and restored a stable capitalist regime). The appearance of governments of this type was foreseen in the "Theses on Tactics" adopted by the Fourth Congress of the

Communist International, and pointed to by Trotsky in the Transitional Program as a possible forerunner of the establishment of a workers state.

While the Nicaraguan workers and peasants government is politically independent of the bourgeoisie, the latter's economic and social power have so far only been weakened. Remnants of the old state structure remain intact. Bourgeois and petty-bourgeois figures hold governmental posts. Capitalist ownership and control over major sectors of industry, commerce, and agriculture have not been broken, which means the class character of the state remains bourgeois.

If this contradiction between workers and peasants government and bourgeois state is not resolved by a thoroughgoing expropriation of the big imperialist and domestic bourgeoisie and repudiation of the foreign debt, the capitalists—backed up by Washington, international finance organizations, and capitalist regimes in Central and South America—will use their economic positions and growing economic hardships to erode the power of the new government, sabotage economic reconstruction, foster division among the toilers, reconstruct their own political and military power, and reverse the revolutionary process initiated by the Nicaraguan masses led by the FSLN.

Cuba and Nicaragua

6. Although the revolutionary process now under way in Nicaragua bears many resemblances to those which occurred under the workers and peasants governments established in Cuba and Algeria, each of these cases has its own particular characteristics.

In Nicaragua, the establishment of a workers and peasants government after the fall of the dictatorship was not preceded by a period of rule by an unstable bourgeois coalition regime. In Cuba and Algeria, on the other hand, the political power and influence of bourgeois governmental figures at the outset of the revolution were greater than in Nicaragua. As a result, in Cuba and Algeria these bourgeois figures felt more confident in openly resisting or balking at purges of the old state apparatus, in opposing the acceleration of mass mobilizations and the accumulation of radical measures aimed at carrying out the programs of the Cuban July 26 Movement and the Algerian FLN. Thus the transition from a bourgeois coalition government to a workers and peasants government in both Cuba and Algeria was marked by changes in the composition of the government as well as by radical measures and mass mobilizations in support of them. In Cuba Osvaldo Dorticos replaced Manuel Urrutia as President. Che Guevara replaced Felipe Pazos as head of the National Bank, and Cuba's ambassador to Washington, Miró Cardona, defected. In Algeria Mohammed Khider, Ferhat Abbas, and other bourgeois leaders were successively ousted.

In Nicaragua, the initial impact of the deepening revolutionary situation was expressed, on the governmental level, in the decisions taken by the FSLN. In light of the class relationship of forces established by the massive urban insurrections, they decided to postpone and restructure the class composition of the Council of State. They created a governmental setup in which all decisive decision-making power from the outset clearly rested in the FSLN's hands, although bourgeois figures participated. This was different from the very first stages of either the Cuban or Algerian postliberation regimes.

In both the latter countries however, as in Nicaragua, bourgeois figures were still in major government posts at the time that the workers and peasants governments came into being. In Cuba, some were not purged until the early 1960s; in Algeria some were never purged.

The acceleration of mass mobilizations and the steady accumulation of anticapitalist measures has certainly met with resistance from the greatly weakened bourgeoisie in Nicaragua. But most Nicaraguan capitalists still fear that an open provocation or head-on confrontation at this time would redound to their detriment. Within the government, bourgeois figures try to use *de facto* veto—as the relationship of class forces allows—over the most radical measures. At some stage this will pass over into denunciatory resignations or recalcitrant obstructionism which will force the FSLN to remove them.

The more consistently radical course of the new Nicaraguan government from its first day (compared to the bourgeois coalition regimes in either Cuba or Algeria) reflects its different nature. Bourgeois figures in those governments carried out antilabor measures and openly attempted to block progressive ones. The bourgeois Supreme Court, basing itself on the 1940 constitution, resisted the Castro leadership's land reform. There were attempts from inside the government to reestablish a bourgeois army. Such moves by the bourgeoisie spurred the class confrontations in Cuba that led to the workers and peasants government.

The greater speed of events in Nicaragua is accounted for primarily by the broadly insurrectional character of the victory there. It accelerated the development of mass organizations of the urban and rural toilers on a scale unmatched in Cuba. Because of the dramatic shift in the relationship of class forces created by this massive upsurge, the FSLN took the opportunity, which it had not previously expected, to conduct a preemptive purge of capitalist political power and set off along a course that radically diverged from its earlier agreements with bourgeois forces in the anti-Somoza opposition.

In Algeria, in a number of big ways, the revolutionary process was much less advanced during the workers and farmers government there than in Nicaragua today. For example, mineral, banking, and insurance sectors remained in private hands and the FLN government did not implement radical currency or trade controls of the type already imposed by the FSLN-led government in Nicaragua.

In Cuba, the conflict between the workers and peasants government consolidated by late 1959 and the bourgeois state was resolved by August-October 1960 with the establishment of a state foreign-trade monopoly, further agrarian expropriations, and the nationalization of virtually all U.S. and Cuban industry. Despite the absence of a Leninist party, the anticapitalist measures carried out by the revolutionary Castro leadership, relying on mass workers mobilizations, could not have been rolled back short of a full-scale civil war backed to the hilt by the massive intervention of Yankee imperialism. A workers state had thereby been established.

In Algeria, on the other hand, the revolutionary process initiated in 1963 with the emergence of a workers and peasants government under Ahmed

Ben Bella was cut short. Unlike the Castro leadership, Ben Bella responded to pressure from the right and accommodated to the demands of French imperialism. The regime turned away from mass mobilizations and from creating a militia and attempted to slow the tempo of change. The foundations of the workers and peasants government began rotting away. When army commander Houari Boumediene took advantage of the vacillating leadership and declining mobilizations to stage a coup in June 1965, the Algerian government changed direction and reversed many of the earlier progressive measures. A capitalist government was put in the saddle. The capitalist state was preserved and subsequently reinforced.

In Nicaragua, the outcome of this fundamental contradiction between the class character of the workers and peasants government and the capitalist state still hangs in the balance. The designation of Nicaragua today as a workers and peasants government in no way implies that a workers state will automatically be the outcome of the process under way. The big class conflicts that will settle that question still lie ahead. As the workers and peasants press forward to win their demands, the imperialists and Nicaraguan bourgeoisie will strike blows. They will have to be met with counterblows. Each new encroachment against capitalist property and prerogatives will meet stiffening resistance by the reaction. Open breaks will occur within the government and all other Nicaraguan institutions.

A workers and peasants government is by its very nature an unstable and transitory formation: It must either *move forward* to the establishment of a workers state, or—failing to decisively break the economic power of the bourgeoisie—*fall back* and open the way to a reassertion of capitalist political power and reinforcement of the bourgeois state. How this unstable situation will be resolved in Nicaragua depends in large part on how well the FSLN responds to the initiatives of the masses and succeeds in educating, organizing, and mobilizing them. They will have to defeat the counterrevolutionary threats. And they must be prepared to face the eventuality of direct U.S. military intervention aimed at preventing the triumph of a second workers state in the Western Hemisphere.

7. The FSLN was formed at the beginning of the 1960s under the impact of the socialist revolution in Cuba. It was able to tap the popular tradition of radical anti-imperialist struggle symbolized by Augusto César Sandino's rebel peasant and worker army in the 1920s and early 1930s.

From its origins, the FSLN was shaped by its strong identification with the experience and Marxist evolution of the Castro-Guevara team, and the Cuban revolution. While of similar social composition to the July 26 Movement, it started out with an advantage—the ability to learn from the example of the Cuban workers state and from the further political evolution, experiences, and false starts of the Castro leadership team. In addition, many FSLN cadres were recruited out of the worldwide youth radicalization of the 1960s and early 1970s and gave more serious consideration to Marxist ideas, including those of Lenin and Trotsky, than the early cadres of the July 26 Movement.

Under the impact of the defeats its guerrilla units suffered in the 1960s and the dramatic growth of the urban proletarian and semiproletarian population in the 1960s and the early 1970s, a discussion developed in the FSLN over an assessment of its guerrilla strategy. This led in 1975 to a division into three tendencies that later became three separate public factions. Their differences reflected debates over the relation of armed struggle and mass mobilizations, the respective roles of the urban and rural toilers, the relation between military and political struggle, and the purpose and acceptable limits of pacts with the opposition bourgeoisie.

In the final analysis, these differences boiled down to contending points of view around a decisive question: *How to topple Somoza and throw off imperialist domination of Nicaragua.* The answer was to be given in practice before the decade was over.

The political content of these debates reflected the ripening objective conditions for the overthrow of Somoza and contributed to the overall political education and development of all three tendencies. Challenged to meet the responsibilities posed by accelerating revolutionary developments, the tendencies reached agreement on unity in action in June 1978 and reunified in December of that year. Their leadership bodies fused and old divisions in the ranks broke down, as the tasks posed by the rising class struggle resolved in life many previously disputed questions.

The FSLN leadership was profoundly affected by the largely unanticipated scope and power of the 1978-79 urban mobilizations and by the spread of popular committees and militias—sometimes at the initiative of the FSLN, often through spontaneous mass emulation. The revolutionary process gave a powerful thrust toward bypassing the bourgeois-coalition government that the FSLN had, on the eve of the insurrection, considered inevitable.

The actual course of the insurrection caused the FSLN to move in an increasingly anticapitalist direction. This course has demonstrated the FSLN's will and capacity to learn from and respond to the actions and aspirations of the workers and peasants. Relying on the organization and mobilization of the masses, the FSLN has led the process that has brought a workers and peasants government into being. This is consistent with its efforts to learn from the Cuban experience.

By learning from the example of the Cuban revolution and Castro leadership, the FSLN bypassed Stalinism and Social Democracy and has been able to carry out an intransigent and victorious struggle against Somoza and his imperialist backers, opening the door to the fight for the second workers state in the Americas.

The advances already registered under the leadership of the FLSN, like the July 26 Movement victory in Cuba twenty years ago, constitute a blow to world Stalinism. The central founder of the FSLN, Carlos Fonseca Amador, broke from the Partido Socialista Nicaragüense (PSN), the Nicaraguan Stalinist party, and the FSLN was built in opposition to the PSN. By bypassing the Stalinists *in action*, the FSLN further deflated the Stalinists' claim to be the only current ever to stand at the head of revolutionary mass upsurges. And by unyielding struggle at the head of the insurrectionary proletarian and plebeian masses, the Sandinistas provided in practice a living alternative to the Stalinist line of "two-stage" revolution in which the interests of the toilers are subordinated to the interests of the bourgeoisie. Thus, the FSLN-led revolution in Nicaragua has strengthened the revolutionary current within the workers movement internationally and has shifted the relationship of forces against the Stalinist camp.

Despite its expressed desire to establish workers and peasants power in Nicaragua, the FSLN leadership has thus far not organized a mass Leninist party that would best insure the positive resolution of the class contradiction between the government and state.

But the direction of the FSLN shows that it would be a grave error to think that any *a priori* limits exist on how far its leadership and cadres can develop and how fast they can act as the class struggle deepens in Nicaragua.

The FSLN has announced its intention to launch a vanguard party rooted in the masses. The construction of a revolutionary socialist proletarian party within which the political vanguard of the Nicaraguan working class can democratically debate and decide the important questions facing the revolution would be a major step in advancing and consolidating the gains of the toilers and expropriating the remaining bourgeoisie.

U.S. Imperialism

8. Yankee imperialism failed in its efforts first to salvage Somoza and then, in the final weeks, to establish Somozaism without Somoza. Washington's attempts through the governments of Costa Rica, Venezuela, Panama, and other Latin American ruling classes to insure installation of a bourgeois-dominated government were no more successful than its proposal for a joint military intervention sponsored by the Organization of American States, or its attempt to base troop-carrying attack helicopters in northern Costa Rica on the eve of Somoza's fall. Dashing the hopes of the U.S. rulers, the government that was consolidated not only included the FSLN, but was one in which the Sandinistas held decisive political power.

The fall of Somoza and rapid consolidation of a workers and peasants government in Nicaragua has had a profound impact in Central America—most dramatically in El Salvador—and the Caribbean. This was a giant blow to imperialism's efforts to isolate the Cuban revolution and bolster capitalist rule south of its borders. Today Washington faces increasing isolation in Central and South America and in the Caribbean.

Washington's incapacity so far to directly intervene militarily in Nicaragua fundamentally reflects two factors: (1) the deep solidarity of the Latin American toilers with the Nicaraguan struggle and consequent political cost for any government too openly identified with U.S. imperialism's counterrevolutionary policies; and (2) the constraints on the direct use of U.S. military might as a result of the post-Vietnam antiwar attitudes and suspicion of U.S. foreign policy goals among American workers.

Despite these initial reversals, however, it is precluded that Washington will passively look on while "another Cuba" is established in its own backyard. It is acutely aware that the deepening of the revolution in Nicaragua has already had profound ramifications in Grenada and El Salvador, and will have further repercussions throughout the Caribbean and Central America.

Imperialism's goal is to contain, stall, disrupt, and, at the right moment, crush the Nicaraguan revolution. Along with the economic cudgels wielded by world imperialism, its two strongest weapons in achieving these goals are: (1) the desire of the Kremlin bureaucracy to avoid any disruption of its diplomatic relations with Washington, the fruit of its overall class collaborationist-policy of peaceful coexistence with imperialism; and (2) Washington's own massive military power.

The U.S. rulers initially adopted an openly aggressive stance toward the revolution. They warned the new government against radical measures and against any close association with Cuba. In this way, the imperialists sought to strengthen the hand of what they had hoped would be a politically viable bourgeois wing in the government. When it became clear that the FSLN was in political control of the government, beginning in late August, big business media, especially in the United States, made a noticeable shift in its treatment of the Nicaraguan events. This reflected imperialism's tactical judgment that use of open force, or the overt threat of open force, could politically backfire in the short run.

News from Nicaragua virtually dropped from the papers and news broadcasts. And editors toned down their earlier dire warnings about the dangers of an FSLN-led government.

Imperialism's tactics up until now have revolved around maintaining an outward appearance of fairness and friendliness toward the new government, while exploiting the economic devastation to arrest and prepare to reverse the revolutionary process. Somoza inflicted massive destruction on the country during his final year in power. More than 35,000 people were killed in the last year alone, and 100,000 wounded. Damage to schools, hospitals, and social services amounted to $80 million. Agricultural production was severely disrupted and 40 percent of the population goes without adequate food. More than half the active population is unemployed, and a quarter of industrial plants were damaged by Somoza's bombs.

All this was superimposed on the growing misery caused by the 1972 earthquake damage (Somoza stole millions of dollars in international reconstruction aid to expand his personal financial empire), by other consequences of the dictator's grand-scale corruption, and by the blows of the world capitalist economic crisis. These economic problems will be exacerbated as an inevitable food crop shortage develops during the early months of 1980.

Taking advantage of this social and economic dislocation, Washington is seeking to limit the flow of aid into Nicaragua to intensify the pressures bearing down on the FSLN-led government and on the morale of the Nicaraguan masses. The Carter administration promises credits, both loans and aid. But aside from some initially limited food aid, they have not given a single penny. At the same time, a certain amount of the aid from its imperialist allies is funneled not to the government but to projects directly strengthening imperialist links with the private sector, thus reinforcing the remaining points of support for the Nicaraguan bourgeoisie. The policy as a whole revolves around buying time for the Nicaraguan capitalists. Washington is counting on the coming economic pressures to alienate the petty bourgeoisie and parts of the toilers and hopes this will gradually demobilize the masses and divide the FSLN itself.

The imperialists are organizing these pressures on Nicaragua through their international financial institutions; their domination of trade and distribution in the world capitalist market; the Latin American bourgeoisies, who desperately fear a new Cuba; and the international apparatus of the Social Democracy, which acts as a political tool of world capitalism, especially for the Western European powers.

By avoiding a public propaganda campaign against the Sandinista revolution, Washington at the same time aims to erode international solidarity with Nicaragua. It wants to project the image that adequate aid is being sent and that there is no danger of imperialist-orchestrated military intervention. It even hopes to foster the knee-jerk sectarian reaction among some radicals that if Washington isn't openly yelping, then the Nicaraguan government must be betraying the masses. Unfortunately, the petty-bourgeois left has largely taken the bait in the United States, the country whose government poses the greatest threat to Nicaragua. Those sectarians that are not already advocating the overthrow of the new government and denouncing the FSLN, are mimicking the low-key coverage of the bourgeois press and abstaining from solidarity efforts.

Meanwhile, Nicaragua's aid needs are *not* close to being met. And there is a real danger of military intervention connected to the coming conflicts with the Nicaraguan bourgeoisie or explosions over the extension of the Nicaraguan revolution.

The U.S. and Honduran governments are aiding and intimately collaborating with the remnants of the Somocista National Guard. Moreover, Washington has launched an aggressive military buildup in the Caribbean and renewed calls for a Latin American "regional military peacekeeping force." By mid-November 1979, Somocista National Guard units, some integrated into the Honduran army, began incursions into Nicaragua to engage the FSLN in battle. The Honduran air force began illegal overflights of Nicaragua. Nicaraguan diplomats faced intense harassment—including arrests and beatings—in the Honduran capital, to such a degree that all personnel but one chargé d'affairs were withdrawn from the Tegucigalpa embassy by the Nicaraguan junta. Washington's silence in the face of the attacks on Managua's emissaries in Honduras stands in sharp contrast to its hue and cry over the events in Tehran in the same period.

Carter's Threats

9. Washington launched a new series of threats against Cuba in September on the pretext that a Soviet "combat brigade" was stationed there. This was linked both with their attempts to discredit Cuba's leadership of the non-aligned conference and with the squeeze on Nicaragua. The Cuban government has responded with enthusiastic solidarity and material assistance to Nicaragua. It has issued an embarrassing challenge to the U.S. government for an emulation competition to see who can provide the most aid to reconstruct Nicaragua. Moreover, Washington knows that Cuba is aiding the new government on the island of Grenada and liberation groups throughout Central America. In a September 30 interview presented for nationwide broadcast over CBS television's "60 Minutes" show in the United States, Castro was questioned about Cuban aid to the opponents of the dictatorship in El Salvador. Castro said: "I neither confirm it nor deny it. I proclaim it as a right; furthermore, as a duty."

Above all, the U.S. rulers know that Cuban aid to Nicaragua helps counteract imperialist pressure and thereby strengthens the ability of the FSLN-led government to reconstruct Nicaragua along socialist lines. They know that the FSLN looks to the Cuban workers state as a model for social and economic development.

Furthermore, in light of Cuba's role in Africa, the imperialists are convinced that Cuba will come to the aid of Nicaragua in the event of a direct U.S. or U.S.-engineered attack, posing a confrontation of international proportions.

Carter's moves in the Caribbean are also a warning to the Soviet Union. Washington is telling the Kremlin that it won't tolerate any substantial Soviet aid to Nicaragua. And it is pressuring Moscow to put the squeeze on Cuba to abandon its internationalist policies, including its aid to Nicaragua.

Cuba has made clear that it won't be intimidated, however. It responded to Carter's moves by asserting that "Cuba's dignity and sovereignty, its right to defend itself by any means it regards as appropriate, as well as its internationalist policy, will remain unshakeable." Castro pointedly included "our sister socialist nations" in his call for an emulation contest to aid Nicaragua.

In contrast to the anti-imperialist policies of the Castro leadership, the Stalinist bureaucracy in the Kremlin seeks to gain trade and diplomatic concessions from imperialism in return for using its power and influence to sabotage revolutionary struggles. So far, Moscow has heeded Washington's warning to withhold major assistance from Nicaragua. And following Moscow's lead, Stalinist parties around the world have given little coverage to the Nicaraguan revolution in their press and have not used their full influence to mount solidarity campaigns.

The aggressive maneuvers by the Carter administration over the past several months, together with Moscow's refusal to provide adequate aid to Nicaragua and its demonstrative support to the new military regime in El Salvador, show that defending Cuba against imperialist pressure and fighting to lift the economic blockade are intertwined with defense of the Nicaraguan revolution.

10. As yet, the Sandinistas still lack the mass democratic-centralist proletarian party that would best enable them to meet the challenges and opportunities they face. Moreover, the FSLN faces huge obstacles: economic dislocation, which will produce great hardships—and class conflicts—in the early months of the 1980s; a shortage of political cadres; the inexperience of the new mass organizations; cultural deprivation imposed by imperialist subjugation; and maneuvers by imperialism and the indigenous capitalists.

Yet the FSLN's course up to now, together with the growing militancy and political class consciousness of the workers, gives no cause for pessimism.

Faced with the threat of imperialist intervention and counterrevolutionary subversion, the Sandinistas have moved rapidly to build a professional revolutionary army, as well as a new police force under FSLN control. It has also announced plans to construct a large workplace-based militia, and draw the CDSs into the fight against rightist terror.

But direct military threats are not the only danger to the revolution. The economy's fundamental economic laws foster capital accumulation and expanding capitalist economic power on the basis of the large remaining blocs of private property in the means of production.

The economic chaos caused by Somoza is the biggest factor operating to the benefit of the exploiters inside and outside Nicaragua. Despite the measures that the government has already taken in health, education, and other areas of social welfare, an austerity situation has been imposed on the country.

As the government has correctly taken steps to revive a minimum of industrial and agricultural production, in the private as well as the public sector, the economic power of the bourgeoisie and the inevitable dangers associated with that power have become more obvious. The capitalists insist on credit and currency concessions, alleviation of trade controls, and assurances that wage demands resulting from the growing unionization of workers will not undercut profitability. A confrontation is looming over these issues.

The bourgeoisie retain their Chambers of Commerce and Industry, which are supported by their counterparts elsewhere in Central America and by international financial institutions. While the bourgeois political parties—the Social Democrats, Social Christians, Democratic Conservatives, and others—presently have a very narrow popular appeal, they nonetheless serve as a vehicle for organizing propaganda campaigns against the government and mass organizations. The Catholic Church hierarchy retains some credibility among the Nicaraguan masses. Sections of it are another potential support for rebuilding bourgeois political power.

The most important bourgeois propaganda instrument in this regard is the country's largest daily, *La Prensa*, though even this is limited by the necessity, given conditions in Nicaragua, for *La Prensa* to open its pages every day to FSLN leaders, laying out the Sandinista perspective or responding to criticisms of policies of the government or FSLN.

The presence of bourgeois figures in the junta and cabinet is not a mere decoration. It is an expression of the fact that the contradiction between the class character of the workers and peasants government and the bourgeois state has yet to be resolved. As the government is buffeted by conflicting class pressures, by the initiatives and counterinitiatives of the toilers and the exploiters, movement toward or away from establishment of a workers state will find its reflection in further alterations in personnel in the junta, the ministries, and the central bank.

It would be a blunder to conclude from this, however, that progress toward a progressive resolution of this contradiction can be furthered by agitation around the slogan, "Bourgeois ministers out of the government!" Such a schema ignores the real location of military and political power, the deep-going character of the break in continuity with the old regime, the progression of radical measures by the new workers and peasants government, and the real process through which the masses will advance their consciousness to drive the revolution forward. It would be infantile leftism to deliberately provoke a premature confrontation with the bourgeoisie over the composition of the junta and cabinet. The decisive conflicts will grow out of the intensification of the class struggle, which will be reflected in the government; as the bourgeois forces in the government make themselves known by their deeds, it will then become timely to fight for their ouster.

Revolutionary Course

The Nicaraguan capitalists face the growing power of the Sandinista army and police, the CDSs, the CST, the ATC, the women's and youth organizations. The FSLN has sought ways to organize their power, including taking more governmental prerogatives. It encourages the democratic organization of these committees on a neighborhood and district level, and has projected the next stage as consolidation on a municipal level. National gatherings of CDS and ATC activists have already been held, and a provisional National Council of the CDSs has been set up. Congresses of CDS and CST delegates are scheduled to be held in early 1980.

The Nicaraguan bourgeoisie, on the other hand, is virulently opposed to attributing any governmental authority to these organizations, insisting that they are merely FSLN bodies. This dispute has become a public debate.

The coordination and centralization of these mass organizations on a municipal, regional, and national level—together with the extension of workers control over all areas of production and economic activity, both privately owned and nationalized—would further weaken the social and economic power of the capitalists and sharpen the class confrontation. Such steps would prepare the way for the establishment of a workers state based on these mass organizations and generalized workers control evolving toward workers management as democratic participation by the toilers in national economic and social planning is established.

Prospects for development toward institutionalized workers democracy along these lines show the sectarian error of placing the demand on the Nicaraguan government to organize the election of a constituent assembly. Those in the radical movement who advance this slogan seek to promote the false idea that the government is a bourgeois coalition regime, or that the FSLN is depriving the masses of their democratic rights in order to reconsolidate capitalist power. However, it is these sectarians themselves who actually counterpose an unfounded schema to the process by which the Nicaraguan toilers have already begun to assert their own power against that of the class enemy. It's no accident that variations on the same theme are one of the complaints hurled by the bourgeoisie against the Sandinistas.

The FSLN's stated intention to develop the mass organizations as the basis for popular power in Nicaragua opens up the most positive framework, as *Barricada* has explained, for the masses to create "their own means of resolving their political, social, and economic problems," "to defend themselves against their enemies, and to consolidate the revolution." It is this dynamic of the revolution that the capitalists will oppose most strongly, demanding that the junta take steps to regulate and hold back the extension of the power of the mass organizations.

11. The success of the FSLN, and the revolutionary workers who join them, in building a mass-based vanguard party will be an extremely important factor in increasing the chances that the workers and peasants government will culminate in the establishment of a workers state that can effectively fight to defend and extend the revolution. No single element is more important to the consoli-

dation of the gains of the revolution than forging a party of the Nicaraguan working class that takes the political leadership in building a centralized system of democratic workers and peasants councils to assume governmental power.

Combating capitalist sabotage and reconstructing Nicaragua will require an ever-wider exchange of viewpoints within the camp of the toilers over how best to move forward to solve their problems. The greatest possible democracy and the cultivation of an atmosphere encouraging the free expression of ideas can only strengthen the revolution and the commitment of the masses to it. It is the only means to tap the full talents of the workers and peasants, who must be drawn into the revolutionary movement in increasing numbers and become the overwhelming bulk of its cadres and leaders.

It is natural that different currents of thought will emerge, even among the most advanced workers collaborating to build their vanguard party. Various tendencies or parties will arise, reflecting the uneven development of class consciousness among the workers. The Sandinistas know from their own experience that tendencies and political differences, even sharp ones, can develop among revolutionists.

Impatience with the serious political errors and often provocative behavior of some sectarian organizations,* however, led the FSLN in September and October to publicly lump these groups together with the Somocistas. During the campaign against right-wing terror launched under the slogan "Control Somocismo—defend the revolution," the "ultralefts" were mentioned in speeches, on the radio, and in *Barricada* as being among the counterrevolutionary forces that had to be smashed. Detentions and other administrative measures were taken against members of some of these organizations, without presentation of proof of any likely or actual crimes that would justify such measures.

By November a modification in the FSLN's approach to the sectarian-led organizations was becoming evident. FSLN leaders announced that evidence now showed that bank robberies previously attributed to MILPAS had been committed by Somocistas posing as radicals. Speeches by some FSLN leaders, while containing contradictory statements, included offers to open a "dialogue" with the sectarian groups. In addition, all of those detained were released.

Nonetheless, there has still been no definitive public political clarification on this important matter by FSLN leaders.

The pro-Moscow Stalinists in Nicaragua, who had always attacked the FSLN itself for being "ultraleft," will continue to push in the direction of stifling workers democracy. Their attacks are in reality aimed at the toiling masses and at all revolutionists—above all the FSLN—since their objective is to arrest the revolution at the "bourgeois democratic stage." Any policy of repression within the workers movement would play into their hands.

Equating Somozaism and counterrevolution with those under the influence of petty-bourgeois pressures and ideas could also lead to an underestimation of the dangers posed by the real class enemy—both among the capitalists who backed Somoza, those who opposed him for whatever reason, and their powerful allies centered in the United States. As the class polarization deepens, it will be the forces of the bourgeosie that spearhead the counterrevolution.

The revolutionary leadership must be able to distinguish between those in the radical movement who operate within the framework of the revolution and those who—and there will be some—desert to the camp of the class enemy and carry out crimes against the revolution.

The problems the Nicaraguan revolution faces and must immediately cope with are real and cannot be waved aside. It is sometimes necessary to make tactical concessions to the capitalists to avert economic reverses and premature confrontations.

The sectarian groups are wrong in their tendency to view such necessary concessions as incorrect in principle or betrayals of the revolution. They are a vital necessity in Nicaragua. At the same time, however, these organizations can sometimes reflect in a distorted way moods of sections of the masses. In order to effectively lead the masses, the revolutionary vanguard should openly explain its considerations to the workers and peasants when it believes concessions are necessary.

An important part of this process of interaction between the masses and their vanguard is politically confronting the ultraleft sectarians and explaining what is wrong with their infantile proposals. Repression cuts across this political clarification, and makes it more difficult to win these cadres to a genuinely revolutionary course.

Furthermore, the workers and peasants will take intiatives that go beyond the leadership's immediate plans. This is one of the keys to all revolutionary uprisings and victories. The leadership's capacity to respond positively to such initiatives to drive the process forward will be a prime element in the consummation of the objectives of the revolution.

The FSLN's contradictory moves this fall toward repression of its opponents on the left stand as an exception to their generally revolutionary course toward the development of mass popular organizations and respect for democratic rights. If this overall tendency prevails, the direction of the Nicaraguan revolution in this important respect will represent a significant advance over revolutionary Cuba. It could also stimulate motion toward the development of democratic forms of proletarian power based on workers and peasants councils in Cuba.

Toward a Workers State

12. Given the desperate economic situation in Nicaragua, a pressing objective of the government has been to restore a minimal level of production in the privately owned industries and on the big and medium-sized farms still in the hands of their owners. It has appealed for aid from all countries to obtain credits and food.

As the example of Cuba has proven, however, the needs of the masses cannot be met if private ownership is maintained in the basic means of production. The laws of capitalist accumulation will distort the country's economy, subordinating real economic development and social betterment to the quest for profits and to imperialist

*The Frente Obrero (Workers Front), the trade-union arm of a centrist group with Maoist origins that earlier had split from the FSLN, was the main target of the antiultraleft campaign. It had an armed wing during the insurrection called the Milicias Populares Antisomocistas (MILPAS—Anti-Somoza People's Militias).

exploitation. This would be the inevitable outcome of the maintenance of a "mixed economy" such as that described in the July 9 GRN program.

Thus the reconstruction of Nicaragua in the interests of the workers and poor peasants makes it necessary to extend workers control of production; shift the tax burden to the exploiters; repulse attempts by the imperialist financial institutions to use foreign debt as a means of pressure; nationalize the remaining privately owned large landholdings, industries, and big firms; develop the CDSs and unions, and widen the scope of their authority; expropriate the imperialist banks and enterprises; establish a monopoly on foreign trade; and thus lay the foundation for real economic and social planning.

It is along this road that the system of capitalist accumulation and labor exploitation can be destroyed. Once the qualitative turning point has been passed, and a workers state established, capitalist property relations could be restored only through all-out civil war, requiring ruthless and massive military intervention by imperialism.

These measures, of course, would mark the final showdown with the Nicaraguan bourgeoisie and its backers in Washington and on Wall Street. The FSLN has correctly acted on the recognition that steps in this direction go hand in hand with, and must be preceded by raising the consciousness and organization of the toilers. The class struggle must be taken into the countryside. The CDSs, CST, ATC, Sandinista army, and the new youth and women's organizations must all be expanded and strengthened. The new militias must be established and trained. The new party must be built. All this requires time, and premature confrontations can set back rather than advance the process.

While it would be adventuristic to try to force the rhythm of the class struggle, it is also true that the pace of polarization and confrontation cannot be controlled by preconceived plans. The tempo will be dictated by the blows and counterblows between the masses and the FSLN on one side, and the exploiters on the other. With each new encroachment against the property and prerogatives of the landlords and business interests, the likelihood grows that some section of the bourgeoisie will throw down the gauntlet. In addition to radical measures by the government, the workers and peasants—suffering under economic burdens, capitalist sabotage, and social dislocation—will themselves take initiatives on the land, in their factories, and in the barrios. This is the historic record of the Russian, Cuban, and every other socialist revolution; there is an accelerating dialectical interplay between the leadership and the initiatives and responses by the masses, often unforeseen by the leadership.

In revolutionary situations above all, history confirms Frederick Engels' observation that when controlled forces are put in motion, uncontrolled forces are inevitably put in motion as well. No amount of political preparation can annul this consequence of the class struggle. Instead, the aim of such preparation must be to increase the self-confidence and readiness of the masses *to respond* to new turns by defending their conquests and propelling their struggle forward. That is where their consciousness, organization, and mobilization will prove decisive. It is correct to make concessions to the class enemy when the relationship of forces leaves no alternative. But the masses must be told the class truth about such concessions, so that they can be better prepared to ward off the concomitant dangers.

All this highlights the need for a revolutionary-Marxist proletarian party to unify and lead the workers and their allies in accomplishing these tasks and defeating their class enemy. Forging the initial cadres of such a party out of the leadership and ranks of the FSLN would not only facilitate the socialist reconstruction of Nicaragua, but would mark an advance for the entire international workers movement in the fight to resolve the historic crisis of proletarian leadership.

13. The revolution in Nicaragua and the political evolution of the FSLN present an enormous opportunity and responsibility for the Fourth International. These developments pose new tests for us as we strive to measure up to our historic task of solving the leadership crisis of the world working class and constructing an international party of socialist revolution. The cadres of the world Trotskyist movement are the irreplaceable nucleus of that world proletarian party. We carry forward the Leninist program and transitional method indispensable to the victory of the toilers over the economic and social catastrophe and nuclear annihilation that will otherwise be brought down on humanity by imperialism.

Due to the crimes and obstructions of the Social-Democracy and Stalinism, however, the construction of a mass revolutionary workers international is a task that is still only at its beginning stage. The development of revolutionary currents that bypass Stalinism such as those in Cuba, and now in Nicaragua, are thus of the greatest importance to the Fourth International and to the further development of our prospects and our revolutionary program.

As Trotsky explained, in the death agony of capitalism *revolutionists of action* will continually emerge out of the class battles provoked by the exploiters' ruthless drive for profits. These fighters will arise not only out of the anti-imperialist struggle, but within the labor movement and other organizations of the oppressed in the imperialist countries. History will judge the Fourth International by our capacity to link up with these currents, integrate ourselves in them, learn from them, and help steel them politically in the program of Leninism, and in that process build the world proletarian party that can take on the imperialists in battle and defeat them.

Along this strategic line of march, we recognize in the leadership of the FSLN fellow revolutionists who have already demonstrated their internationalism, their desire to move forward to a socialist Nicaragua, and their intention to build a vanguard party. On that basis, the Fourth International seeks political collaboration with them on all the big questions facing the workers of Nicaragua and of the entire world.

This course runs directly counter to that taken by several organizations that consider themselves Trotskyist—by the Bolshevik Faction, by the Socialist Workers Organization of Costa Rica (OST) and its Nicaraguan sister organization, Revolutionary Socialist Group (GRS), and by the Revolutionary Marxist League (LMR) in Nicaragua. Boiled down to its essentials, the political line of all three of the above has been opposition to the new Nicaraguan government as a bourgeois government and the construction of political parties in opposition to that projected by the FSLN.

The Simón Bolívar Brigade (BSB), established under the direction of the Bolshevik Faction, carried this sectarian line to the point of criminal adventure—sending to Nicaragua and maintaining there an armed unit outside the discipline of the new revolutionary army or the people's militia. The BSB falsely portrayed itself as an FSLN unit in order to win popular sympathy. As a result, the FSLN leadership—after attempting to persuade the BSB to take its place among the forces striving to advance the revolution and respecting revolutionary legality—expelled the Brigade's non-Nicaraguan members.

Having been called to order by leading bodies of the Fourth International for its utterly undisciplined and disloyal course, which was not conceived to advance the interests of the workers and peasants of Nicaragua, the Bolshevik Faction organized a split on the eve of the International's World Congress. It has been joined in this walkout by the leadership of the Nicaraguan LMR and the Costa Rican OST, and is now attempting to organize a rump "world conference" with other sectarian groups internationally that call themselves Trotskyist and who share a sectarian disdain for and lack of comprehension of the Nicaraguan revolution.

The Fourth International condemns and repudiates the activities of the Simón Bolívar Brigade and rejects the political views on the Nicaraguan Revolution of the Bolshevik Faction, the LMR, and the OST. The Fourth International has no organized forces in Nicaragua—the activities of the latter groups have been organized outside the guidance of, or collaboration with, the elected leadership bodies of the Fourth International. As mentioned earlier, these groups have now split from the Fourth International. The policies of these groups are diametrically opposed to those of the Fourth International and can only harm the opportunities to win a hearing for Trotskyist ideas in Nicaragua and advance our international party-building perspective.

Partisans of the Fourth International present their ideas as loyal and hard-working militants in the framework of the organization that led the overthrow of Somoza and is today guiding the revolution forward.

By advancing our program and perspectives, the Fourth International places itself firmly on the side of the FSLN's battle to promote and achieve the victory of the socialist revolution in Nicaragua. Our main contributions in this regard are:

• Active participation inside and outside Nicaragua in efforts to reconstruct the country and defend the revolution from all its enemies, above all U.S. imperialism;

• Advancing the development of the unions, of mass organizations and of democratic workers and peasants councils to bring the masses into decision-making and strengthen the revolution; and

• Loyal participation in the FSLN's efforts to construct a revolutionary proletarian party, putting forward the fundamental program of Leninism in order to advance toward the mass world party of socialist revolution whose construction will be decisive in the defeat of exploitation and oppression on an international scale.

Aid to Nicaragua

14. Outside Nicaragua, the Fourth International and its sections will mobilize all their forces to build broad, united solidarity and aid campaigns with the Nicaraguan revolution and help defend it against the threat of imperialist-orchestrated counterrevolution. Part of this will be a campaign against the blockade and other hostile acts against revolutionary Cuba. We will energetically work with others to involve the labor movement, farmers organizations, organizations of oppressed national minorities, women's groups, youth organizations, and others in a vast effort to publicize the truth about what's happening in Nicaragua and mobilize solidarity and aid with the Nicaraguan people.

This is an especially important responsibility for members of the Fourth International in Latin America, where the direct impact of the Nicaraguan revolution is the greatest, and in the United States, which not only installed and maintained the Somoza tyranny in power but today represents the most powerful enemy of the revolution. In placing ourselves in the front ranks of such a solidarity and aid campaign, the Fourth International will help revive the example of proletarian internationalism demonstrated by the worldwide movement against the imperialist war in Vietnam.

We will demand that the imperialist governments provide whatever economic, agricultural, and medical aid is asked for by the Nicaraguan government—channeled through the official government and mass organizations and with no strings attached. We will back up Commandante Daniel Ortega's proposal before the United Nations that Nicaragua's burdensome debt should be assumed "by the developed countries, by the economically powerful countries, and especially those that fed Somozaism with financing." That means demanding that the imperialist governments and all imperialist financial institutions cancel all of Nicaragua's debts.

The Fourth International calls on the mass workers and farmers organizations throughout the world to make resources available to aid their Nicaraguan brothers and sisters.

We know that political and material solidarity can be decisive to the outcome of the revolutionary process in Nicaragua. The FSLN's steps to encourage the development of such an international campaign show that it too recognizes this fact.

The Fourth International also understands that the socialist revolution that has begun in Nicaragua is an important breakthrough in combatting the isolation of Cuba and hastening revolutionary prospects throughout Central and South America and in the Caribbean.

Finally, we know that the establishment of the second workers state in the Western Hemisphere would further weaken world imperialism, inspire and educate the oppressed and exploited around the world, and buy precious time for the workers in the advanced capitalist countries to take political power out of the hands of the warmakers and exploiters and open the road to a peaceful and prosperous socialist future for all humanity.

15. The outcome of the deepening confrontation of class forces in Nicaragua will profoundly affect the Cuban workers and peasants and the outlook of their leadership. The future of the two revolutions are now inextricably linked.

The establishment of a workers state in Nicaragua would make possible another huge step forward in the struggle to resolve the crisis of leadership of the world proletariat. It would have an immediate, positive impact inside Cuba, and its weight would be felt throughout the Caribbean and Central America. It would spur the development of revolutionary forces, and strengthen them in their conflict with Stalinist and Social Democratic betrayers, and centrist vacillators.

As a result, the door would be opened further to a process that could lead the Castroist leadership, the FSLN, and other revolutionists linking up with the Fourth International in steps toward building a mass world party of socialist revolution.

The Fourth International must prepare for the showdown that is approaching in a matter of months. Decisive moves towards the establishment of a workers state in Nicaragua will entail a head on confrontation with the Central American bourgeoisies and the power of Yankee imperialism. The leadership of the Cuban revolution will face one of its biggest tests since the missile crisis of 1962. Every current claiming to be revolutionary will be tested to the end.

Today it is the heroic workers and peasants of Nicaragua who are on the front lines of the advancing world socialist revolution. We will be tested by our capacity to respond with courage and decisiveness, to throw our forces into the struggle without hesitation or delay, to mobilize and lead all those we influence. Only along that road can we advance the construction of the world party of socialist revolution.

The New Rise in the World Class Struggle

by Steve Clark

[The general line of the following report was adopted by the Socialist Workers Party National Committee May 24, 1980. It is reprinted from the *ISR* section of the June 20, 1980 issue of the *Militant*.]

* * *

During the last four months the working class and its allies have struck further blows against world capitalism.

At its World Congress last fall, the Fourth International, the world party of socialist revolution, took note of the shift in the world relationship of class forces against imperialism—above all U.S. imperialism—and in favor of the oppressed and exploited. The Socialist Workers Party noted the same development at our convention last summer. The short period since these meetings has been marked by an acceleration of that process, tipping the scales further in our direction.

In the past two months alone, there have been *four* anti-imperialist demonstrations of more than a million people—one in Iran, in response to Washington's threats, and three in Cuba. The latest of them—the May 17 March of the Fighting People—mobilized nearly half Cuba's population. And in Nicaragua—which only has a population of around 2.5 million—250,000 workers and peasants turned out for May Day in Managua.

Going back a bit further in time, there have been *two* massive urban revolutionary insurrections in one year: in Tehran in the winter of 1979; and in Managua and other Nicaraguan cities that summer.

And just this week, hundreds of thousands of workers and students in South Korea took over the city of Kwangju and a score of nearby towns for several days in opposition to a tyrannical military dictatorship. This comes at the crest of a wave of strikes and protests throughout the country over the past month. And as the events in Kwangju show, the crisis of the South Korean military regime is deepening.

Taking events back still further to the 1975 Vietnamese triumph over the U.S.-backed Saigon dictatorship, we can point to other victories in Africa, Spain, Kampuchea, Afghanistan, the Mideast, and Grenada.

But for the purposes of this report, we want to push our time frame even further back. Back to two guideposts that can help us gauge how far our class has come in the past two decades; and to get ready for the period of sharpening battles at home and abroad that we are heading into—in particular, the showdown and very real prospect of war in the Caribbean and Central America.

These two guideposts are:

1) The victory of the Cuban Revolution in 1959-60; and

2) The opening of a new stage of the world revolution in 1968-69 with the beginning of a process of radicalization of the working class of the imperialist countries. This process deepened as a result of the 1974-75 worldwide recession and capitalist austerity offensive, and it continues to unfold today.

At the last meeting of the SWP National Committee in January (see "The Crisis of Imperialist Domination" in the *ISR* section of the February 15 *Militant*), we took a close look at what we called the crisis of the world imperialist system—the struggle of the oppressed nations against the oppressor nations, and the growing weight and centrality of the working class in these battles. Now we need to tie in the conclusions of that report with the crisis of the world capitalist system—with the class struggle and relationship of forces *inside* the major capitalist countries. Because the period we have now entered is being shaped by the reciprocal effects of these crises.

What factors have made possible the big strides by the toilers of Nicaragua, Iran, Afghanistan, Indochina? It is not only the courage and tenacity of these anti-imperialist fighters, but the accelerating political and economic changes *inside* the imperialist countries, especially the United States. What the bourgeois pundits call the Vietnam Syndrome—the unwillingness to fight capitalism's wars to put down colonial rebellions; the skepticism of U.S. foreign policy; the resistance to an indefinite future of sacrificing for something called the "national interest"; the growing suspicion that the "interests" at stake are *not ours*.

The Cuban revolution

Let's start with the Cuban Revolution.

Due to the post-WW II Stalinist betrayals of revolutionary possibilities in Western Europe, and the subsequent twenty-year period of overall capitalist expansion, center stage in the world revolution in the 1950s and much of the 1960s was almost entirely occupied by the colonial revolution. Petty bourgeois nationalist and Stalinist leaderships predominated, as did peasant forces and struggles more often based in the countryside than in cities.

The Cuban revolution marked a historic turning point.

For the first time since the Bolsheviks, the Stalinist and Social Democratic misleaders and bourgeois nationalists were bypassed by a revolutionary current—and by one that took power and established the first workers state in the Americas.

The Socialist Workers Party recognized the significance of this event at the time. In the document our party submitted in 1963 "For An Early Reunification of the World Trotskyist Movement," we noted that "The Cuban Revolution dealt a blow to the class-collaborationist policy of Stalinism in Latin America and other colonial countries. New currents, developing under the influence of the victory in Cuba, are groping their way to revolutionary socialism and seeking to apply the main lessons of the colonial revolution to their own situation."

And we drew attention to two important results of this development:

• *first,* that it would increase the "effectiveness of our defense of the colonial revolutions within the imperialist countries"; and

• *second,* that it would give "added weight" to the "program of Trotskyism" among "serious revolutionists who seek the fundamental . . . transformation of their countries."

For us and for the world working class, the most important thing was that in the course of the battle against Batista and U.S. imperialism, a new Marxist leadership began to be forged.

We hammered away at the significance of Cuba over and over again. Pathfinder publishers has just reprinted *Che Guevara Speaks* with the two-page preface that Joseph Hansen wrote for it in 1967. After pointing to the inspiration that Che had provided to the new generation of radical youth, Hansen noted that:

"Something bigger even than Che is involved—the Cuban revolution and its contribution toward solving the most crucial single problem facing humanity: the construction of a leadership capable of guiding the way out of an economic order reeking in every pore with corruption, filth and blood."

Che, Fidel, and "the team they built," Hansen continued, "appeared on the scene, evidently as forerunners of a great new development in world politics—the rise of a generation of revolutionary fighters disinclined to accept either Moscow or Peking or any similar center as a kind of Vatican that in practice serves to stultify both revolutionary theory and practice."

Che, he said, was "representative of a new type destined to become more and more numerous, a *revolutionist of action. . . .*"

The Castro team had developed from petty-bourgeois revolutionists into leaders "committed to the socialist goal, whose outlook converged more and more with the classical revolutionary Marxist tradition that stood behind the October 1917 Russian Revolution."

While recognizing the historic significance of this new development, we also understood the limitations imposed by the continuing lag both in the postwar political awakening of workers in the advanced capitalist countries and in the involvement of the urban proletariat in struggles in the semi-colonial countries.

The Cuban revolution represented a sharp break with the previous period of postwar history; but it also arose out of and was shaped by that period, and before all the elements of a new world political situation had begun to crystallize, as they soon would.

There was a gap. That generation of revolutionists had begun to obtain a scientific understanding of the class struggle by reading the Marxist classics, and from studying the experience of previous generations. But there was nothing in their own direct experience that demonstrated in life the strategic role of the industrial working class in leading the fight against capitalist rule and the conquest of political power.

This was not only before the first stirrings of class battles in the imperialist centers, but before the 1969 revolt of the masses in Cordoba, Argentina, that helped bring down an earlier military dictatorship in that country; before the Popular Assembly established by the Bolivian labor movement in 1971, before the *cordones industriales*—committees in factories and working class neighborhoods—took shape in Chile in 1972-73, and before huge urban mobilizations in 1974 brought down Haile Selassie in Ethiopia, before the Soweto uprising in South Africa—and, of course, before Iran and Nicaragua.

This gap, in turn, was largely responsible for some of the central political limitations of the new Castroist current: its tendency to underestimate, or even ignore, and write off for this historic period, developments in the working class of the imperialist countries; and its raising the tactic of rural guerrilla warfare to the level of a *strategy* for extending the revolution, to the detriment of the *strategy* of Leninist party building and participation in the broad working-class movement and organizations.

The transition out of this initial postwar situation—a transition opened by the Cuban revolution—was brought to a head by the Vietnam War, another development with a foot both in the past and future. It was a largely peasant-based, anti-imperialist struggle under a Stalinist leadership. But the impact of Vietnam's heroic resistance on the economic and political situation in the United States and other imperialist countries helped usher in a new stage of the class struggle in those countries. These direct results of Vietnam coincided with and were exacerbated by the exhaustion of the motor forces of the long capitalist expansion.

This brings us to our second guidepost.

Rise of Workers Struggles

By 1968-69, there were unmistakable signs of a percolation of the class struggle in Western Europe, North America, and other imperialist countries. Workers struggles began to rise once again in Europe, following a youth radicalization spurred by identification with the colonial revolution. The May-June 1968 general strike in France—which began from a police attack on a student anti-Vietnam War protest and widened to decisive sections of industrial workers—and the wave of labor battles that kept Italy in prerevolutionary turmoil in 1969, were indicative of these changes.

In the United States, a break-up of the Cold War political stability preceded the shocks of the world economic crisis. The Black struggle—itself inspired by the colonial revolution—and the growing opposition to the U.S. slaughter in Indochina sparked a broad political radicalization among young people that challenged many of the "sacred cows" of U.S. imperialism—anticommunism, "my country right or wrong," racism, the inequality of women, and so on.

At the same time, the Vietnam-fueled inflation was rapidly undermining the strength of the dollar on which world trade had been based since the late 1940s. For the first time since the end of the war, workers began to feel a pinch, rather than a gradual rise, in their real wages.

And this was brought home with a vengeance in 1973 with the price explosions, especially in oil and gas—the beginning of the energy crisis. Following on the heels of this was a worldwide recession—in this country, the worst since the 1937 depression.

The bosses the world over were driving to solve the crisis of *their* system, *their* profits, by taking it out of *our* hides. This has led to a growing realization by workers that things are not going to get better, they're going to get steadily worse. And as this month's big strike and lock-out in Sweden illustrate, this reality is shaking up even world capitalism's showcase of class peace.

These important developments flowing from the economic crisis of world capitalism are increasingly converging with—affecting and being affected by, shaping and being shaped by—the political crisis of the world imperialist system.

Another important effect of the capitalist crisis is its disastrous impact on the imperialist-distorted economies of the semi-colonial countries. This, in turn, has profound political results. We've seen the effects of austerity plans imposed by the International Monetary Fund on Peru, Egypt, Zaïre, and Turkey. We've seen the results of the growing scissors between the world market prices of the commodities these nations export and the prices of those they must import, especially oil.

Today, the political impact of this squeeze is being felt in Jamaica—right in the midst of a revolutionary upsurge swirling all around it in the Caribbean. The imperialist bankers and their political front-men in Washington have told the Manley government that it won't get a cent of desperately needed loans unless it drives through yet another austerity campaign. Given the build-up of social tensions as a result of earlier imperialist-dictated austerity measures, Manley was forced to say no this time; and now the CIA is at work with its Chile-style "destablization" tactics, including terrorism and sabotage, as the September elections there draw near.

Origins and Limits of Détente

From the standpoint of the imperialists, the beginning of the convergence of the political and economic crises of its world system took sharp form at the beginning of the seventies in the political, military, and economic quagmire Washington found itself in over the Vietnam War. With no prospects of a military victory, and with political and economic costs at home intensifying, the U.S. rulers turned to the Stalinist bureaucratic castes in Moscow and Peking for help to dig themselves out—and got it. That was the beginning of "détente."

Détente was rooted in the *weakening* position of U.S. imperialism, its need to carry out a major tactical retreat to regroup its forces and to enlist the Stalinist bureaucracies to help buy the time to do that.

In a 1973 report to the SWP National Committee on "The Unfolding New World Situation," SWP National Secretary Jack Barnes described the imperialists' attempts to develop a new strategy.

He noted an important factor "which the American rulers may not see clearly enough to incorporate adequately into their strategy." That factor was that détente "will not guarantee maintenance of the status quo."

"The most elusive culprit remains the built-in contradictions of the capitalist system," he said. "That is the one 'subversive' they can never put in jail."

Three years later, in a report on "The Erosion of World Stalinism," Barnes again stressed that "the very prize that both American rulers and the Soviet bureaucracy are after—stability, class peace, maintenance of the status quo—is exactly what détente cannot produce for them."

By that time, this assessment had already been confirmed in the victories in Vietnam and Angola, the fall of the Portugese dictatorship, and Watergate.

In the four years since that report was given, it

has been borne out time and again. If ever there was a period that illustrates what we mean by saying that the two main actors on the world stage are the capitalist ruling classes and the exploited classes—*not* the ruling classes and the Stalinist and social democratic bureaucracies—this has been such a period. Détente has been rocked to its foundations, and its built-in limits exposed by the irrepressible conflict between the classes.

Intended by the imperialists to bail them out of Vietnam, détente worked for several years—but the struggle broke through again in 1975. The Indochinese revolution had been slowed down but not defeated. And the imperialists had to flee Saigon in helicopters.

The Indochinese revolution has continued to show its power, despite U.S. imperialism's economic blockade and military pressure. The workers state initially limited to North Vietnam was consolidated throughout the country in mid-1978; the Pol Pot dictatorship fell before Vietnamese troops and Kampuchean insurgents in early 1979; and there have been further advances in Laos; the Thai dictatorship has been shaken; and Washington's "China Card" was trumped last year when Peking's attempt to "punish" Vietnam for its role in Kampuchea ended in what is today acknowledged to have been a military and political disaster. The proposal in some capitalist quarters earlier this year that Peking could somehow be of direct military aid to the U.S.-backed rightists in Afghanistan was quickly put on the shelf.

Détente has also failed to produce the hoped-for results in Africa. The reverberations of its 1976 setback in Angola are still being felt today in the big mobilizations that have occurred in Zimbabwe; the retreat that the imperialists and white-settler regime there have been compelled to accept; the prospects for further steps toward dismantling the racist white-settler system in Zimbabwe; and the weakening of South African control over Namibia and the stability of the apartheid regime itself.

In the Mideast, the tenacity of the Palestinians, the instransigence of Zionism, and its ruthless policy of establishing and defending settlements on the West Bank, and above all the shockwaves of the Iranian revolution, have blown apart Washington's hopes of drawing other regional capitalist regimes into the Camp David framework. The Iranian revolution inspired the toilers throughout the region, intensified their hatred of U.S. imperialism, and created a situation where even the most reactionary regimes—such as those in Saudi Arabia, Jordan, and even Pakistan and Turkey—must take some distance from Washington out of fear of the consequences among the masses of their own countries.

The outbreak of the revolution in Afghanistan in April 1978 is another clear example of how the class struggle has undermined détente. This revolution was something that neither the U.S. rulers *nor* the Soviet bureaucracy wanted or expected; but the revolution began despite them. The efforts of Washington to halt the revolution and place a U.S.-backed regime in power there, posing a new imperialist military presence right on the borders of the Soviet Union, finally forced the Kremlin—for its own reasons and with its own bureaucratic methods—to intervene on the side of the new regime against the reactionary coalition of landlords, capitalists, tribal chieftains, and heroin smugglers.

The resulting sharpening of class conflict in the area, combined with the increasingly aggressive U.S. military pressures against Iran, forced the Kremlin to tone down its condemnations of the occupation of the U.S. embassy in Tehran and begin to offer assistance to Iran in the event of imperialist economic sanctions. This, of course, ups the ante around any new U.S. military moves in Iran.

All this happened not because Washington and Moscow wanted it to happen; to the contrary, they wanted stability and class peace. But the revolutions in Iran and Afghanistan upset the apple cart.

No Alternative Strategy

In reality, the imperialists have no strategy to replace the Cold War policies of containment and rollback. They have been left to muddle through from crisis to crisis, hoping they could rely on the bureaucracies to hold back struggles, or on help from client regimes such as that of the shah and Somoza. They have tried to buy time in order to turn around the balance of forces at home and abroad that prevents them from using their own massive military might against the world revolution.

This is what they are looking for every opportunity to do today—around the recent Indochina wars, the hostages in Iran, the Soviet intervention in Afghanistan, and now around Cuba and the Caribbean. They are constantly probing, and this back-and-forth struggle has become a central axis of U.S. politics today—a battleground between the rulers who need to militarize the country and the majority of U.S. working people who "don't want to kill or be killed for Exxon." The blows that the U.S. rulers have been dealt from Angola through Nicaragua have deepened the Vietnam Syndrome."

The syndrome is an international one, as well. The European and Japanese workers don't want to go to war either. They aren't happy about having Pershing II nuclear missiles scattered around their countries by NATO. They don't want to go to war with the Soviet Union or Iran. They face inflation, layoffs, and cutbacks, and aren't in any mood to sacrifice still more so that their governments can meet Carter's demand to shoulder more of the burden for financing imperialism's war machine.

The resistance by the U.S., European, and Japanese workers to the war plans of the world's most powerful capitalist ruling classes is opening even more doors for the exploited colonial masses.

And the imperialists have learned from Iran and Nicaragua—and they see the handwriting on the wall in South Korea today, too—that these semi-colonial client regimes, even the strongest of them, are in no shape to use their armies as surrogates for imperialism against the colonial revolution. Only the imperialist outposts such as Zionist Israel and apartheid South Africa are of substantial help to Washington and its major allies. And that's why—whatever secondary tactical dispute might arise—the U.S. and European rulers will back these reactionary regimes, arm them to the teeth, and do everything possible to ensure their survival.

The Cold War was not something that the imperialists turned off for awhile and can simply turn back on again. It reflected the relationship of class forces that came out of World War II, both inside the imperialist countries and worldwide.

And that balance of forces has been radically changed by world events. It was based on the long capitalist expansion, and U.S. imperialism's preeminent position in it; on Washington's initial big military advantage over the Soviet Union and China because of its nuclear arsenal; on the domestic situation in the United States, marked by witch-hunting, anti-communism, and a housecleaning and housebreaking of the American trade unions through the strengthening of the bureaucracy's stranglehold. All these conditions cannot be put back together by the capitalists, short of a major defeat for the workers in the United States, other imperialist countries, and the semi-colonial world.

So, when we correctly say that détente has been seriously weakened, we must remember that the imperialists have no alternative to détente right now. As they prepare to restore their capacity to use their military power, they will still turn to the bureaucracies for help—just like the employers still try to use the class-collaborationist union officialdom as they gear up for an all-out antilabor drive.

And Moscow and Peking still base *their* perspective on deals to shore up the international status quo.

What has changed, and changed radically, are the estimates—all the way around—of what détente can produce and the recognition of its growing limits because of the strengthening of the workers and farmers on a world scale.

The Castro Leadership

This is the situation that Wall Street, Washington, and the Pentagon face as they desperately search for ways to untie their hands for counterrevolutionary action around the world.

Into this breach—marked by a rise of revolutionary struggles and a weakening of the mainstay of world counterrevolution—has stepped the Castro leadership. Unlike the Moscow and Peking Stalinists, they never bought their way into détente—despite their deep need to end the U.S. economic blockade and their standing offer to normalize diplomatic relations with Washington. The U.S. rulers refuse to even discuss these matters unless Cuba first pulls back from its internationalist activities in solidarity with anti-imperialist struggles.

Despite this, the Cubans have stood shoulder to shoulder with those in struggle against U.S. imperialism in Angola and Ethiopia, in Indochina, in Southern Yemen.

And the key confrontation has been in U.S. imperialism's own backyard—Central America and the Caribbean.

The deaths over the past several years of Mao Tse-tung in China and, just recently, President Tito in Yugoslavia were more than simply the deaths of two individuals. They should have symbolized the death of any illusion that these two leaderships, by charting a course away from the Kremlin, had provided a revolutionary road forward for the workers of the world.

Tito and Mao broke from Moscow. But they never broke from Stalinism—from class collaboration, from the myth of socialism in one country, from deals with imperialism at the *expense* of the world revolution.

That explains the extremely sympathetic treatment of Tito in the big business press. The *New York Times* called him a "giant among Communists." And Carter hailed him as "a towering figure on the world scene."

Can anyone imagine that the death of Fidel Castro would evoke the same response? Tito began earning these rave obituaries back in 1950 by backing the imperialist intervention in Korea. And his last political act "on the world scene" was to cooperate with Pol Pot, with the capitalist dictatorship in Singapore, and with other neocolonial regimes to oppose the anti-imperialist line of the Cubans at the Non-Aligned Conference in Havana last September.

Impact of Workers Struggles

In contrast to the Chinese and Yugoslav Stalinists, the Castro leadership has had a revolutionary internationalist perspective from the outset. And this internationalism has been deepened, and infused with a clearer class content, by the rise of the world revolution during the past half decade, by the growing weight of the proletariat in these battles, and by the new opportunities for the Cuban government to act and make a difference.

The Cubans themselves testify to the inspiration and invigoration they have drawn, especially from the extension of their revolution in the Western Hemisphere. Early in the events around the Peruvian embassy, I was struck by one particular paragraph in a front-page editorial in *Granma*:

The editorial warned that Washington would be badly misjudging the Cuban people if it believed they would fail to defend revolutionary Cuba or struggles elsewhere in Latin America:

"We have resisted heroically for 21 years," *Granma* said, "and our enemies must resign themselves to the idea that we will resist until the final victory of the sister peoples of our hemisphere—"

And then—as if to show that more than bravado and wishful idealism was involved—the editorial added, "especially now that we are not alone!"

The socialist revolution in Nicaragua, the new Grenada, the reverberations in El Salvador and throughout the region—this is what the Cubans have been banking on and working for for twenty-one years: the extension of the socialist revolution in the Americas, a breakthrough, despite all the attempts of Washington to isolate and strangle the Cuban revolution.

The Castro leadership has also been affected by developments in the class struggle in the imperialist countries. The Cuban leaders talk more in *class terms* about the *entire* world than they did in the past. We've seen Castro's recognition in his opening address to the Non-Aligned Conference of the "important role the people of the United States played" in ending the Vietnam War; his appeals during his United Nations address to workers in the advanced capitalist countries, pointing out how they too suffer from the inequities of the existing world economic order.

The failure of rural guerrilla warfare as a strategy in Latin America; the rise in the weight of the working class and urban centers in the semi-colonial world; the centrality of mass urban insurrections in the Iranian and Nicaraguan victories; the big workers struggles in Brazil and their beginning revival in Pinochet's Chile; the role of the Bolivian workers last fall in blocking a military coup, arms in hand—all these factors have also had an impact on how the Cuban leaders understand and orient to various social forces in the battle against imperialism.

And it has affected the way they understand and explain the success of their own revolution, as well.

More and more often during the past several years, the Cuban leaders have found opportunities to tell the story of the urban underground in Cuba; the role of Frank Pais; Celia Sanchez's roots in this front of the revolution; the decisive role of the workers after January 1959 in mobilizing to defend the gains of the revolution and carry it through to its completion.

Right now, both the Cubans and our party have our eyes fixed firmly on the same thing: the gigantic class confrontation that is shaping up as the revolution picks up steam in the Caribbean and Central America and the imperialists seek ways to crush it, ways to reassert their military might and strike a blow at the oppressed and exploited throughout the world.

This is an enormous political question for us. The American workers are the biggest obstacle to Washington carrying out its counterrevolutionary plans in the Caribbean. Whether conscious of it or not—and most aren't yet conscious of it—the U.S. workers are the invaluable and irreplaceable ally of the Central American and Caribbean revolution. And if Carter succeeds in defeating anti-imperialist fighters anywhere in the hemisphere, it won't only be those fighters who will pay a heavy price; it will mean death and sacrifice for American workers too.

Let's take a look at what is happening in Central America and the Caribbean today.

Revolution Deepens in Nicaragua

First, Nicaragua. There has been a major deepening of the revolution and class polarization there. These events confirm the correctness of the assessment adopted at the January 1980 plenum of the SWP that:

• a workers and farmers government had come into existence in Nicaragua sometime in the month or so following the powerful July 19 insurrection that toppled Somoza; and

• the FSLN, *by its actions*, had shown itself to be a leadership of revolutionary caliber. (See "Revolution in Nicaragua," in the February 1 *Militant.*)

Just since the turn of the year:

• The ambitious literacy crusade has begun, involving—both as students and teachers—a big percentage of the Nicaraguan population. The result will be not only important strides toward teaching more than half the adult population how to read and write for the first time, but giving them an education in class politics, preparing them as class conscious fighters.

• The government has expropriated substantial new tracts of land and put them under the direction of the agrarian reform ministry and the Sandinista-led Rural Workers Association (ATC).

• Workers at privately owned factories have taken over production and demanded government intervention against employers who are sabotaging production or draining capital from the country. And the government has backed these workers up. The Sandinistas have pointed to the key role of workers control in combatting sabotage, meeting the country's reactivization goals, and preparing for greater involvement of the workers in setting the course of the revolution.

• With the Sandinista Peoples Army formed, the volunteer militias have begun to be organized based in the workplaces, schools, and countryside.

• Solidarity with El Salvador has been organized throughout the country. FSLN leaders make clear that the Sandinista army, militia, and police will take up arms against any outside aggression against El Salvador.

• FSLN leaders have traveled to the USSR and Eastern Europe, where they obtained agreements for trade, technical assistance, and other aid.

Most recently, there has been the announcement of the decisive worker-peasant majority in the Council of State, which began its sessions at the beginning of May. Representatives of the mass organizations—unions, neighborhood committees, women and youth organizations, peasant and agricultural workers organizations—these are the majority in this governmental institution. According to the composition initially outlined in the July 1979 Program of Government, the council was to have had a decisive capitalist majority. The plans to establish that kind of bourgeois-dominated parliamentary body as a brake on the revolution were laid to rest by the powerful insurrection that brought the Sandinista-led masses to power July 19. The FSLN, basing itself on the mandate of that powerful revolutionary uprising, blocked the convocation of the council with its original composition. They announced that it would be restructured along more democratic lines to reflect the true balance of class forces in revolutionary Nicaragua.

The Sandinistas' firmness in carrying through this pledge—the fact that they *do* what they *say* they are going to do—was seen by all classes in Nicaragua as a clear signal of the revolution's political direction. This leadership bases its policies on defending and promoting the class interests of the workers and peasants.

The resignation from the junta by Alfonso Robelo reflected the assertion of the interests of another class, the capitalist class. Robelo claimed "excessive" Cuban influence over the revolution. He charged that there were too many Soviet diplomats in the country. And he denounced the make-up of the Council of State as "totalitarian."

A council with a decisive majority of the landowners and capitalists—that's democracy to Robelo and his class. A council with a decisive majority of forces that speak for the interests of the toiling majority—that's "totalitarianism." What more classic statement of the perspective of liberalism?

Despite the presence of figures such as Robelo in the junta, the Nicaraguan capitalist class exercised no governmental power. Following July 19, the Sandinistas moved decisively to construct a new revolutionary army and police, prevent convocation of the bourgeois-dominated Council of State, and consolidate their own political power and that of the mass organizations.

The FSLN's consistent use of political power to promote mass mobilizations and implement measures giving top priority to the interests of the toilers confirmed the government's character as a workers and peasants government.

Robelo, Violeta Chamorro, and a few other non-FSLN figures had achieved a certain reputation among layers of the Nicaraguan masses because of their opposition to the Somoza dictatorship. The Sandinistas chose to let some of these figures demonstrate their actual class allegiances by how they responded to the deepening of the revolution's anticapitalist direction. In this way, those who openly began to oppose the policies of the government exposed themselves before the Nicaraguan people.

On the economic level, the Sandinistas have followed a similar policy. Not yet ready to directly administer the entire economy, the government has told many capitalists that so long as they cooperate in relaunching production and helping to rebuild the war-shattered economy, they will not be expropriated. Meanwhile, the Sandinistas have encouraged the expansion of workers control to prepare both the government and working class to operate the entire economy.

The result has been that the FSLN has consolidated its mass support to meet the inevitable bourgeois resistance to the course of the revolution—either in the form of economic sabotage or political maneuvers.

When the composition of the Council of State was announced, Robelo showed his true colors. He sought to use the false charge of "totalitarianism" to hide his real aims.

But the Sandinistas responded by explaining the conflicting *class* interests at stake. The day after Robelo's resignation, Commander Bayardo Arce, speaking for the FSLN's National Directorate, explained that "the essence of the problem lies in the fact that Robelo could not identify himself with a political platform that limits indiscriminate enrichment and benefits the dispossessed majority of the country."

The deepening of the revolution has led to growing disarray and tactical differences among the remaining bourgeois forces in Nicaragua, as well as a division of labor. For example, the bourgeois parties are boycotting the Council of State, while the Superior Council of Private Enterprise (COSEP) is participating.

When the FSLN last week appointed two new figures to the junta to replace Robelo and Chamorro—the previous head of the central bank and a supreme court judge—COSEP challenged the right of the Sandinistas to choose the replacements. At the same time, it demanded that the junta reaffirm "the concept of private property and provide protection against" the expropriation of land and factories, warned that the "government's deviations threaten to reproduce in Nicaragua a communist dictatorship similar to Cuba," and threatened that this worsens "the climate of confidence—already damaged—that the urgent reactivation of the country requires."

In other words, if you don't meet our demands, we won't produce.

The FSLN has already stated its position on such blackmail: The 1980 economic plan will be implemented with the private sector, without the private sector, or against the private sector. It's up to them.

So, the confrontation is mounting on this level, as well.

The resolution that we adopted at our last plenum pointed out that: "The decisive conflicts will grow out of the intensification of the class struggle, which will be reflected in the government. The bourgeois forces will make themselves known by their deeds," we said.

This was confirmed by the Robelo resignation, and again last week when José Francisco Cardenal—chosen by COSEP to fill one of the Council of State's three vice-presidencies—defected to the United States after holding that seat for only ten days. At a press conference in the U.S. capitol building, he said that the Sandinista revolution has an "irreversible tendency toward a Marxist-Leninist system" and is "taking control of the means of production by expropriating land and factories."

He denounced other capitalist sectors for "collaboration" with the Sandinistas. "Some of them are acting in good faith, romantically," he said. "Others are doing it thinking that they are gaining time, with the hope that unpredictable events can prevent a catastrophe; and still others with criminal premeditation, thinking that they will get rich in the process."

Well, the Political Committee of the Socialist Workers Party agrees with Cardenal on at least one question: given the events of the last months and the performance of the Sandinista leadership, we are convinced that the direction of the Nicaraguan revolution is irreversible, short of a defeat as the result of a civil war backed by imperialist military intervention.

The FSLN has shown by its deeds that it is a revolutionary leadership consciously preparing and mobilizing the working masses to become the rulers of society. The stage has been reached in this process that the workers and farmers government, resting on the deepening mobilization and class consciousness of the masses, cannot now be overthrown through a process of erosion, but only through an imperialist-backed military attack.

Nicaragua is now in the process of the establishment and consolidation of the second workers state in the Americas.

Extension of Revolutionary Leadership

What is so important for us is not merely the extension of the socialist revolution, but the extension of a revolutionary socialist leadership. Not merely the fact of the revolution, but how the revolution has unfolded, and the perspective of its leadership toward further extending the revolution. *For the first time since the Bolsheviks,* a leadership has come to power that not only bypassed the Stalinists and Social Democrats, but *from the outset sought to organize and mobilize the working class to make a socialist revolution.* This is different even from the Cuban experience twenty years ago, where the socialist direction of the revolution grew empirically out of the determination of the leadership to carry out a thoroughgoing anti-imperialist revolution, no matter what the capitalists or Washington had to say.

This is not because the Sandinistas are better than the Castro leadership, but because they took power in a different historical period. They stood on the shoulders of the Cubans, having been trained and educated by the example of the Cuban workers state and its leadership. Their road is the Cuban road and it—in turn—is becoming a new model for all of Central America and the Caribbean.

At every step the Sandinistas have relied above all on the mobilization and organization of the workers and peasants, systematically educating them in class-consciousness and class struggle.

They have recognized that a revolution is not an administrative operation; it cannot be imposed. They have organized the most politically conscious layers of the toilers to bring along the less conscious—through things like the literacy campaign, the unionization drives, mass rallies, and so on. They have sought to integrate the Indian-speaking populations of the Atlantic coast into the revolution, conducting the literacy drive in the language they speak as well as Spanish, and guaranteeing their cultural integrity.

Of course, they have made mistakes in handling certain situations, especially in their relations with various ultraleft sectarian and Stalinist currents in the workers movement: the way they explained the shutdown of the newspaper *El Pueblo* and the moves against the Frente Obrero, Nicaraguan Communist Party (PCN), and the union federation led by the PCN, the CAUS.

Even on these questions, however, the Sandinistas have acted not from the bureaucratic, totalitarian mentality of Stalinists trying to hold back the revolution and keep a tight rein on power and privileges. They have attempted to grapple with problems thrown up by the revolution, by the unevenness of consciousness among the masses, by the enormous objective difficulties confronting the country.

And they have shown a remarkable capacity to learn from and correct past errors. For example, in the Council of State, five of the eight seats alotted to trade-union confederations were given to unions that are not FSLN-led; this includes one seat to the CAUS. This represents a significant, even if partial, recognition that these unions do have a base among certain sectors of the workers, and that achieving unity on the trade-union level is a political task, not one that can be imposed from above based on the Sandinistas' political authority.

The FSLN's ability to handle such problems is hampered by the break in the historical continuity of Leninism. This break is due to the Stalinist distortions of the true history of the October 1917 Russian revolution and its lessons, as well as to the small size and influence of our world movement, which has preserved that continuity.

This historical break means that revolutionists of action such as the FSLN are sometimes destined to approach certain political problems as if these are entirely new problems without the class-struggle traditions that could help orient them in developing correct solutions.

Class-Struggle Explanations

The significance—from the standpoint of solving the worldwide crisis of proletarian leadership—of the emergence of the Sandinistas and their collaboration with the Castro leadership in Cuba is not only reflected in what they have *done,* and how they have conducted themselves, but also in how they *explain* what they did and what they intend to do.

This marks a big step toward Marxism, toward a revolutionary working class perspective and world movement for our class internationally.

An interview with FSLN commander Humberto Ortega appeared earlier this year in the English-language *Granma,* the organ of the Cuban Communist Party. This interview showed that the FSLN is grappling with the question of the role of the working class; of the urban mass movement; of the need for a party to make and lead a socialist revolution.

". . . we always took the masses into account, but more in terms of their supporting the guerrillas, so that the guerrillas as such could defeat the National Guard," Ortega said. "This isn't what actually happened. What happened was that it was the guerrillas who provided support for the masses so that they could defeat the enemy by means of insurrection." He explained how the insurrection, general strike, and military struggle had been coordinated in the final months.

Ortega also noted, significantly, that "It would have been very difficult for us to win by depending only on internal developments."

"The international balance of forces," he said, "the international situation, the state of the various forces in the area, the contradictions of the Western developed countries, etc., must definitely be taken into account."

This process of thinking—dealing with many of the same questions of revolutionary strategy that are at the heart of our conception of the workers and farmers government—was also expressed in the FSLN's "Balance Sheet of the Revolution" published at the end of December in its *Poder Sandinista* weekly:

"In a revolution we must make a distinction between taking power and exercising that power," it said. "When we speak of power we must also distinguish between class instruments (the army and administration) and class power (what interests those instruments defend).

". . . yesterday the government defended the oppressing and exploiting classes," it said, "while now it defends the interests of the oppressed and exploited classes of Nicaragua. And defense of this government means increasing the workers' participation in all economic, social, political and ideological decisions of the revolution, both national and international."

The point here is not the correctness of every line, word, or formulation, but the tendency of this current to tackle the big problems of the revolution and counterrevolution from the standpoint of the line of march of the working class and its historic clash with the interests of the exploiters, both the domestic and the imperialist monopolists.

As the revolution has deepened, of course, it has more and more become a target of the bourgeois press.

One of the clearest examples was in the London financial weekly the *Economist.* Its special correspondent in Managua could barely restrain his class horror at what was happening.

"Trade unions, peasant groups, and Cuban-style Sandinista defence committees in each neighborhood have been springing up like mushrooms," the *Economist* reported.

It's all well and good to teach people how to read and write, the article said, "But some ask why literacy is getting a priority higher than those of rehousing the homeless victims of the civil war, fighting widespread malnutrition. . . ." It is touching to see the *Economist* suddenly so concerned about the food and shelter of Nicaraguans!

Then, the reporter offers an answer to his own question about why literacy is getting top priority. And he is clearly not happy about it:

"From the first sentence to be learnt 'Carlos (sic) Sandino guide of the revolution' to the last

"The Sandinista are the vanguard organization of the Nicaraguan people'—there is scarcely a phrase that does not ram the Sandinista message home. The reader is taken through eulogies to land reform, to nationalisation and to 'peoples power.' At the end of the campaign, many peasants may know no more than how to scribble and shout a handful of political slogans."

Or perhaps how to read, write, and think for themselves a bit better and about how to advance and defend the interests of their class.

As a positive alternative, the *Economist* quotes Robelo: "I want Nicaragua to be a social democracy like Costa Rica, maybe more to the left of Costa Rica." And then the clincher: "I don't want it to be another Cuba."

This concern with the entire unfolding of events in Central America was also conveyed in the headline of a recent *New York Times* editorial: "The Fire Next Door."

It's not only Fidel Castro who recognizes that "Grenada, Nicaragua and Cuba are three giants rising up . . . on the very threshold of imperialism."

It was no accident that Fidel singled out these three—and pointed to El Salvador as the possible fourth. Fidel has various lists for specific occasions: sometimes Jamaica gets prominent mention, or Panama, or Guyana, or Mexico, or—until recently—even the Andean Pact countries or Costa Rica. All these regimes have had run-ins with Washington that, at one time or another, have impelled them to open up a crack in the solid wall of boycott and nonrecognition imperialism has tried to throw up around Cuba.

But to the Cubans, Grenada, Nicaragua—and they hope soon El Salvador—fit into another category, a category of anti-imperialist and social revolutions, part of their political current.

Revolution in Caribbean

The *Militant* and *Intercontinental Press/Inprecor* have been giving substantial coverage to the revolution in Grenada. They've sent correspondents there to get a first-hand view of these important events and report them back to the readers of our press.

Like Nicaragua, the Grenadan revolution is a development that the U.S. rulers hate with every ounce of their class instinct for survival. A recent article on Grenada in *U.S. News & World Report* was headlined, "Serpent in Caribbean's Island Paradises."

The government that came to power there following the March 1979 revolution, led by the New Jewel Movement, has followed a radical course. It has acted to promote the interests of the workers and peasants, organize and mobilize them, and free the island from imperialist subjugation.

The New Jewel Movement explicitly points to Cuba as a model for the Grenadan revolution, and it has followed the anti-imperialist line of the Cuban leadership on major questions of international politics, defying the imperialist bully to the north. Grenada is receiving essential help from Cuba in setting up an army and militia, as well as badly needed economic, medical, and educational assistance.

At the huge May Day rally in Havana, Grenada's Prime Minister Maurice Bishop was among the featured speakers. ". . . we recognize in Grenada . . . that without the Cuban revolution of 1959 there could have been no Grenadan revolution, nor Nicaraguan revolution in 1979," he said.

Despite the small size of Grenada, it is destined to play an important role in the confrontation that is coming in the Caribbean. If the imperialists touch Cuba or Nicaragua, Bishop said, "they touch Grenada too."

The Grenadan revolution will have an especially big political impact on revolutionary-minded workers and youth in those Caribbean countries with large Black populations—Haiti, St. Lucia, Dominica, Jamaica, Martinique, Guadaloupe, and others.

And developments there are being followed closely by militant Blacks in this country, as well.

El Salvador

Over the past year, under the impact of Nicaragua, there has been a big rise in the class struggle in El Salvador. All the class forces there recognize that an urban insurrection is on the agenda, that the country is on the edge of a civil war. The revolutionary groups have growing popular support and exercise predominant influence over major unions, peasant committees, and other mass organizations.

Washington has made clear that it won't allow 'another Nicaragua.' Of course, it didn't 'allow' the first Nicaragua, either. It simply wasn't able to stop it.

Just as Washington ended up hanging onto Somoza and Somozaist forces to the bitter end in Nicaragua, it is backing to the hilt the military-civilian junta in El Salvador and the junta's policy of *real* repression with *phony* reform. Washington is providing arms, military advisers, money, helicopters, and other forms of direct assistance already.

Washington doesn't feel confident right now that it can directly intervene militarily against the revolution in Nicaragua. The Carter administration is even still steering the $75 million loan package through Congress.

Instead, Washington is preparing to make its stand around El Salvador. And it is already spreading the rumor of "outside intervention" by Cuba and Nicaragua to provide a cover for its own intervention, as well as a cover to use the El

Salvador events to strike out against Nicaragua and Cuba. We can bet that any moves Washington makes to "salvage moderation and democracy" in El Salvador will be coupled with moves to "combat subversion" from Nicaragua and Cuba.

The Colombian regime has taken an openly hostile attitude toward Nicaragua, and last fall withdrew its ambassador from Cuba for being too collaborative with the Cuban government. Venezuela, like Peru, has provoked tensions around the question of Cuban emigration, as well as funneling support to the repressive Salvadoran junta.

These are the governments—the Andean Pact governments—that Castro in his May Day speech called the "political Mafias in this hemisphere." Fidel said that instead of them, Cuba would welcome "a progressive Andean Pact, or better yet a revolutionary Pact . . . the real Pact of Bolívar and of Sandino."

He then listed the sins both of omission and commission by these regimes—on the Cuban blockade, Guantánamo, El Salvador, Puerto Rican independence, Iran.

For us in this country and in the Socialist Workers Party, that speech is one of the most important that Castro has ever given. Not primarily because it answered point by point the imperialist lies and slanders around the Peruvian embassy and the emigrants—although it did that devastatingly well and in a way that is the polar opposite of how Stalinist-led regimes have handled the question of emigration.

But what is most important for working-class revolutionists in this country is to absorb what Castro was saying about the stakes in this hemisphere today, about the battles that are on the agenda. The Cubans are preparing for a showdown with U.S. imperialism over the extension of the socialist revolution in this hemisphere.

Showdown in Caribbean

The May Day speech was a follow-up to Castro's International Women's Day address. At that time, he warned the U.S. rulers not to create "a new Vietnam" in the Caribbean, but that if they did, that's exactly what they would get—a new Vietnam.

The Cubans recognize the big obstacles that Washington faces in using its military might, just as we do. But they are convinced that the imperialists, despite their problems, are dead serious about stopping the spread of the revolution in the Caribbean. The Solid Shield 80 U.S. naval maneuvers in the Caribbean in May, and the planned marine landing at Guantánamo were "a practice invasion" of Cuba, Fidel said. He announced a major expansion of the militias in Cuba, as well as a training program to prepare all Cubans for the eventuality of a total blockade of food and fuel.

The Castro leadership is responsible in its attitude toward the Cuban workers and peasants. It does not raise false alarms. It clearly believes that Washington may well go to war to prevent the revolution in El Salvador. And the Cuban leaders—along with the Nicaraguans and Grenadans—are announcing to the world that they will fight. They will not stand by and allow Washington to crush a revolution.

The sustained mobilizations in Cuba over the past month and a half are intended to prepare the Cuban masses to meet any danger, to inspire and embolden them, to explain and re-explain Cuba's revolutionary internationalist policies—and to give Washington some pause for thought. Given the revolutionary fighting will of the Cuban people, Fidel said, it would be much easier for a foreign army to enter the island than to leave it!

"It's not good to make comparisons with anyone," Fidel said, "it is never pleasant," but "no other revolution has the strength of militant masses that the Cuban revolution has."

That's why, with revolutions on the rise in the Western Hemisphere, Cuba becomes a special target for the imperialists, the target of provocations and slander campaigns. Imperialism "wants the peoples to lose faith in Cuba; it wants peoples to get discourged about the example of Cuba."

Never was there a clearer confirmation of the Castro leaderships' perspective of *extending* the socialist revolution as the only way of *defending* the socialist revolution.

"Do you know what really makes us strong—us, and Nicaragua, and Grenada?" he asked the crowd. "The fact that these are people's revolutions, revolutions with deep roots, with great popular support."

"We have the duty to struggle to develop peace and collaboration between peoples," he said. "But we will never do it by getting on our knees at imperialism's feet to beg for peace."

That is the stance of a revolutionary proletarian internationalist.

Solidarity with Iran

Castro also spoke about Iran, which he called "a real people's revolution" that has "extraordinary force."

"It is our duty to support Iran," Fidel said, "to solidarize ourselves with Iran, because everything that is taking place in Iran reminds us of what happened in our own country."

He also called on the OPEC governments not to sell oil to any country that follows Carter's economic sanctions against Iran.

"This is the time for OPEC to show what it is made of," he said, "to show that it wasn't created just to raise prices and amass huge fortunes. This is the trial of fire for OPEC, the nonaligned countries, and the countries of the Third World."

What was Fidel doing in making this point, just as he did in his remarks on the Andean Pact nations of Latin America? He was drawing a *class line* in the anti-imperialist struggle, in the nonaligned movement, in the colonial and semi-colonial countries. When Cuba and Nicaragua and Grenada *say* something they're ready to *do* something about it—that was Fidel's message.

He was demonstratively charting a way forward for the oppressed masses throughout the semi-colonial world. He was giving voice to *their* anti-imperialist sentiments and to *their* demands against the vacillating, hesitating, and capitulating bourgeois governments that are so afraid of their own peoples that they slink for shelter to the imperialists.

The Cuban leaders have correctly assessed the aborted Carter raid on Iran in the same world political context that we have used in our press. Of course, we don't know, and may never know, exactly what was planned, what went wrong, and exactly why it had to be called off. We may never unravel all the lies.

But clearly a broader military operation was planned. It could have ended in the deaths of many hostages and many Iranians, fighting in Tehran, air raids, and major destruction.

The target was the Iranian revolution. And an obvious objective was further destabilizing the current capitalist government in Iran, which has been unable to stop the advance of the revolution. A goal of Carter's policy is to lay the basis for an eventual coup to put in place a more reliable regime. The imperialists hope such a regime could—with U.S. help—drown the revolution in blood.

Whatever the exact scenario, however, it suffered a major setback that has further undermined any hopes by the capitalists of bringing the revolution to heel in the near future.

The revolution continues to deepen. As the large May Day demonstration in Tehran shows, the shoras (workers' committees) in the factories continue to function. They are raising radical anticapitalist and anti-imperialist demands, and fighting for greater workers control.

The oppressed nationalities have not been crushed. The leaders of the Kurds in particular have shown remarkable political clarity in placing their struggle in the framework of the Iranian revolution, the conflict with imperialism, and opposition to the reactionary military probes and demagogy by the Iraqi regime. They have appealed for support to all the toilers of Iran.

Of course, what is missing so far—and here is is a crucial difference with the Cuban revolution—is the development of a revolutionary socialist leadership to take the revolutionary process in Iran forward to a workers and farmers government. But it is a powerful, deep-going revolution, as have been earlier revolutions in Iran. The revolution in 1906 was not finally crushed until 1911; the one that erupted in 1945 was not ultimately defeated until the CIA-backed coup of 1953 that put the shah back on the throne.

So we can be confident from what we see happening in Iran and from the weakening of imperialism that it will take time to wear down this popular uprising, too. The question will be whether a proletarian party can be forged in time.

The aim of Carter, of course, is to make that period as brief as possible, to cut the revolution short and drive it back, to reassert imperialism's military power in that part of the world, just as it needs to do in the Caribbean.

This parallel has not been lost on the Cubans. The Cubans have offered both political and material support, if Iran requests it.

The main *Granma* article on the Iran events made the correct point that: "Iran is not an isolated case."

The analysis in the *Granma* article compared strikingly to our view of what has been happening in the world class struggle: "In the last few months the Carter administration has initiated a drive to make up for the large-scale defeats suffered by imperialism all over the world. Thus, it intervenes along with China in operations against the Socialist Republic of Vietnam and People's Kampuchea, and it aids and encourages the counterrevolutionary bands in Afghanistan in order to prevent the consolidation of the popular government in that country. It campaigns against the people of Iran and maneuvers with Israel and Egypt to neutralize the Palestinians and other progressive Arab forces, supplies arms and money to Morocco for its colonial war against the people of the Sahara, intervenes against the patriots in El Salvador and promotes vile campaigns against the Cuban revolution, and supports and protects racist and reactionary regimes everywhere."

Getting Ourselves Ready

This convergence between our view of what's coming in the class struggle today with that of the Cubans is important for two reasons:

First, as Fidel explained on May Day, there can no longer be any security for Cuba in the accord reached by Washington and Moscow following the 1962 Missile Crisis, where the U.S. government agreed not to invade Cuba in return for withdrawal of the Soviet missiles. That means that the stakes are very high.

And it places a big responsibility on us. We can be sure that from the outset of any military aggression by Washington, there will be active opposition in this country. This opposition will reach into the factories where we work. It will affect our co-workers, who are not ready to fight in "another Vietnam." It will have an impact on the trade-union movement, and will even be reflected in sections of the officialdom. Any act of aggression by the United States will be extraordinarily unpopular among Puerto Rican, Chicano, and other Latin workers.

It will be particularly unpopular to the growing number of Blacks who will draw inspiration from the revolution in Grenada—a revolution with a Black leadership that speaks in English about the class struggle.

Here, our work in solidarity with Nicaragua, in solidarity with El Salvador, getting out the truth about Cuba and the Central American revolution through the *Militant* and *Perspectiva Mundial* will have laid an important groundwork for us to mobilize opposition to whatever moves the rulers make against these revolutions.

Second, the events in Central America and the Caribbean today are crucial to us because of the revolutionary caliber of the leadership. A new, attractive revolutionary current is developing there under the impact of the Cuban example. In Cuba itself, these events have enormously strengthened the position of the revolutionary Castro wing against the Stalinists, against bureaucratic and conservative attitudes, against those Raúl Castro has called the "fainthearted."

We are watching the development of this leadership and they will be watching what we do and have to say. We will all be in the same trenches against imperialism in the battles that are on the agenda, and fighters always like to know who it is they are fighting next to because it becomes a survival question under the test of class combat.

This is what the Cubans, Nicaraguans, Grenadans, and Salvadorans are preparing for.

And this is what the Socialist Workers Party is getting ready for, too.

Education for Socialists Series

The Workers and Farmers Government
by Joseph Hansen. $7.00

For a Workers and Farmers Government in the United States
by Jack Barnes. $7.00

The Nicaraguan Workers and Farmers Government
by Jack Barnes. $6.00

Marxism and the Working Farmer
by Doug Jenness, with documents and speeches by Frederick Engels, V.I. Lenin, and Fidel Castro. $7.00

Proletarian Leadership in Power
What We Can Learn from Lenin, Castro, and the FSLN
by Mary-Alice Waters. $6.00

Grenada: A Workers and Farmers Government
by Steve Clark. $6.00

Class, Party, and State, and the Eastern European Revolution
$7.00

The Chinese Revolution and Its Development. $8.00

Maoism vs. Bolshevism
The 1965 Catastrophe in Indonesia, China's "Cultural Revolution," and the Disintegration of World Stalinism
by Joseph Hansen.
$10.00

Workers and Farmers Governments since the Second World War
by Robert Chester. $6.00

The Organizational Character of the Socialist Workers Party
1965 resolution of the SWP. $5.00

The Structure and Organizational Principles of the Party
by Farrell Dobbs. $6.00

Pathfinder Was Born with the October Revolution
Three Reports (1991-98) by Mary-Alice Waters. $8.00

Background to "The Changing Face of U.S. Politics" and "U.S. Imperialism Has Lost the Cold War"
by Jack Barnes, et al. $6.00

Background to "The Struggle for a Proletarian Party"
Articles by Leon Trotsky and James P. Cannon. $6.00

In Defense of Revolutionary Centralism
by Jack Barnes. $5.00

1999 Preface to "The Changing Face of U.S. Politics"
by Mary-Alice Waters. $4.00

The Abern Clique
by Joseph Hansen. $6.00

The Revolutionary Perspective for the United States
Theses on the American Revolution
by James P. Cannon. $6.00

Aspects of Socialist Election Policy
edited by Doug Jenness. $10.00

James P. Cannon: A Political Tribute
Including five interviews from the last year of his life. $7.00

James P. Cannon: The Internationalist
by Joseph Hansen, appendices by James P. Cannon. $6.00

Countermobilization: A Strategy to Fight Racist and Fascist Attacks
by Farrell Dobbs. $8.00

The Fight against Fascism in the U.S.A.
Forty Years of Struggle Described by Participants
by James P. Cannon, et al. $8.00

What Is American Fascism?
Writings on Father Coughlin, Mayor Frank Hague, and Sen. Joseph McCarthy
by James P. Cannon and Joseph Hansen. $8.00

From Mississippi to Boston
The Demand for Troops to Enforce Civil Rights. $6.00

Selected Speeches of Fidel Castro. $14.00

Fidel Castro on Chile. $12.00

Revolutionary Cuba Today
The Record of a Debate by Larry Seigle, et al. $12.00

Bolshevism and the Russian Revolution: A Debate
by Doug Jenness and Ernest Mandel. $8.00

Two Study Guides on Lenin's Writings
by Steve Clark and John Riddell. $3.00

Study Guide to "Lenin's Struggle for a Revolutionary International". $5.00

Communist Continuity and the Fight for Women's Liberation
Documents of the Socialist Workers Party, 1971-86.
Edited by Mary-Alice Waters. 3-volume set, $30.00
Women's Liberation and the Line of March of the Working Class (Part I). $10.00
Women, Leadership, and the Proletarian Norms of the Communist Movement (Part II). $9.00
Abortion Rights, the ERA and the Rebirth of a Feminist Movement (Part III). $11.00

Independent Black Political Action (1954-78)
The Struggle to Break with the Democratic and Republican Parties
by Mac Warren. $8.00

The National Black Independent Political Party
An Important Step Forward for Blacks and Other American Workers by Nan Bailey, et al. $5.00

Selected Articles on the Labor Movement (Recent Trends)
by Farrell Dobbs. $5.00

Selected Documents on SWP Trade Union Policy (1972). $5.00

Class Struggle Policy in the Rise of the Labor Movement
by Tom Kerry. $5.00

Defense Policies and Principles of the Socialist Workers Party
by George Novack. $5.00

Against Violence within the Workers Movement. $5.00

Revolutionary Strategy in the Fight against the Vietnam War
by James P. Cannon, Farrell Dobbs, Jack Barnes, et al. $10.00

Israel and the Arab Revolution. By Gus Horowitz. $7.00

Towards a History of the Fourth International
16-volume set, $95.00
(individual volumes available, write for listing and prices)

The Development and Disintegration of World Stalinism. $9.00

Healy's Big Lie
The Slander Campaign against Joseph Hansen and George Novack
by Joseph Hansen, et al. $10.00

Marxism versus Ultraleftism
The Record of Healy's Break with Marxism
edited by Joseph Hansen. $15.00

The US rulers' political crisis and working people's response

Are they rich because they're smart?

Class, privilege, and learning under capitalism

JACK BARNES

$10. Also in Spanish, French, and Farsi.

The Clintons' anti-working-class record

Why Washington fears working people

JACK BARNES

$10. Also in Spanish, French, and Farsi.

Is socialist revolution in the US possible?

A necessary debate among working people

MARY-ALICE WATERS

$10. Also in Spanish, French, and Farsi.

"When we face new and unexpected challenges we will always be able to recall the epic of Angola with gratitude, because without Angola we would not be as strong as we are today."

–Raúl Castro
May 1991

Cuba and Angola: The war for freedom

HARRY VILLEGAS ("POMBO")

$10. Also in Spanish.

Our history is still being written

The story of three Chinese Cuban generals in the Cuban Revolution

ARMANDO CHOY, GUSTAVO CHUI, MOISÉS SÍO WONG, MARY-ALICE WATERS

$17. Also in Spanish, Farsi, and Chinese.

ALSO FROM PATHFINDER

The Rise and Fall of the Nicaraguan Revolution

JACK BARNES, LARRY SEIGLE, STEVE CLARK

Based on ten years of socialist journalism from inside Nicaragua, this issue of *New International* magazine recounts the achievements and worldwide impact of the 1979 Nicaraguan revolution. It traces the political retreat of the Sandinista National Liberation Front leadership that led to the downfall of the workers and farmers government in the closing years of the 1980s. Documents of the Socialist Workers Party. In *New International* no. 9. $16. Also in Spanish.

Socialism on Trial

Testimony at Minneapolis Sedition Trial

JAMES P. CANNON

The revolutionary program of the working class, as presented in response to frame-up charges of "seditious conspiracy" in 1941, on the eve of US entry into World War II. The defendants were leaders of the Minneapolis labor movement and the Socialist Workers Party. Includes Cannon's answer to ultraleft critics. $16. Also in Spanish, French, and Farsi.

Their Trotsky and Ours

JACK BARNES

To lead the working class in a successful revolution, a mass proletarian party is needed whose cadres, well beforehand, have absorbed a world communist program, are proletarian in life and work, derive deep satisfaction from doing politics, and have forged a leadership with an acute sense of what to do next. This book is about building such a party. $16. Also in Spanish, French, and Farsi.

Abortion Is a Woman's Right!

PAT GROGAN, EVELYN REED

Why abortion rights are central not only to the fight for the full emancipation of women, but to forging a united and fighting labor movement. $6. Also in Spanish.

Women in Cuba: The Making of a Revolution within the Revolution

VILMA ESPÍN, ASELA DE LOS SANTOS, YOLANDA FERRER

The integration of women into the ranks and leadership of the Cuban Revolution was inseparably intertwined with the proletarian course of the revolution from the start. This is the story of that revolution and how it transformed the women and men who made it. $20. Also in Spanish and Greek.

Selected Articles on the Labor Movement

FARRELL DOBBS

"Militant workers need both a clear program and a sound strategy. Central to that fight is to politically arm workers to carry the class struggle to the governmental plane by creating their own political party."

—*Farrell Dobbs*

Articles from the *Militant*, written in the mid-1960s. $5

50 Years of Covert Operations in the US

Washington's Political Police and the American Working Class

LARRY SEIGLE, FARRELL DOBBS, STEVE CLARK

How class-conscious workers have fought against the drive to build the "national security" state essential to maintaining capitalist rule. $12. Also in Spanish and Farsi.

The Jewish Question

A Marxist Interpretation

ABRAM LEON

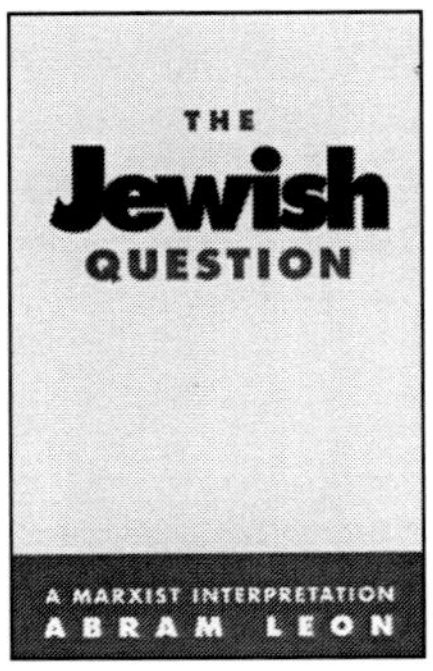

Traces the historical rationalizations of anti-Semitism to the fact that, in the centuries preceding the domination of industrial capitalism, Jews emerged as a "people-class" of merchants, moneylenders, and traders. Leon explains why the propertied rulers incite renewed Jew-hatred in the epoch of capitalism's decline. $25. Also in Greek.

Malcolm X Talks to Young People

"The young generation of whites, Blacks, browns, whatever else there is—you're living at a time of revolution," Malcolm said in December 1964. "And I for one will join in with anyone, I don't care what color you are, as long as you want to change this miserable condition that exists on this earth." Four talks and an interview given to young people in the last months of Malcolm's life. $15. Also in Spanish, French, Farsi, and Greek.

Lenin's Final Fight

Speeches and Writings, 1922–23

V.I. LENIN

In 1922 and 1923, V.I. Lenin, central leader of the world's first socialist revolution, waged what was to be his last political battle—one that was lost following his death. At stake was whether that revolution, and the international movement it led, would remain on the proletarian course that had brought workers and peasants to power in October 1917. $20. Also in Spanish and Greek.

"It's the Poor Who Face the Savagery of the US 'Justice' System"

The Cuban Five Talk about Their Lives within the US Working Class

How US cops, courts, and prisons work as "an enormous machine for grinding people up." Five Cuban revolutionaries framed and held in US jails for 16 years explain the human devastation of capitalist "justice"—and how socialist Cuba is different. $15. Also in Spanish, Farsi, and Greek.

Thomas Sankara Speaks

The Burkina Faso Revolution, 1983–87

Under Sankara's guidance, Burkina Faso's revolutionary government led peasants, workers, women, and youth to expand literacy; to sink wells, plant trees, erect housing; to combat women's oppression and carry out land reform; to join others in Africa and worldwide to free themselves from the imperialist yoke. $24. Also in French.

The Communist Manifesto

KARL MARX AND FREDERICK ENGELS

Why communism is not a set of preconceived principles but the line of march of the working class toward power, "springing from an existing class struggle, a historical movement going on under our very eyes." The founding document of the modern revolutionary workers movement. $5. Also in Spanish, French, Farsi, and Arabic.

Cosmetics, Fashions, and the Exploitation of Women

JOSEPH HANSEN, EVELYN REED, MARY-ALICE WATERS

How big business plays on women's second-class status and economic insecurities to market cosmetics and rake in profits. And how the entry of millions of women into the workforce has irreversibly changed relations between women and men—for the better. $15. Also in Spanish and Farsi.

Teamster Politics

FARRELL DOBBS

How Minneapolis Teamster Local 544 combated FBI and other government frame-ups in the 1930s; organized the unemployed; and fought to lead labor and its allies on an independent working-class political course. $19. Also in Spanish.

EXPAND YOUR REVOLUTIONARY LIBRARY

Capitalism's Long Hot Winter Has Begun

JACK BARNES

Published as the storm clouds of the 2008 financial crisis were forming, Barnes explains that today's global capitalist crisis is but the opening stage of decades of economic, financial, and social convulsions and class battles. Class-conscious workers, he writes, confront this historic turning point for imperialism with confidence, drawing satisfaction from being "in their face" as we chart a revolutionary course to take power. In *New International* no. 12. $16. Also in Spanish, French, Farsi, Arabic, and Greek.

How Far We Slaves Have Come!

South Africa and Cuba in Today's World

NELSON MANDELA, FIDEL CASTRO

Cuban internationalists "made a contribution to African independence, freedom, and justice, unparalleled for its principles and selfless character," said Nelson Mandela, speaking in Cuba in July 1991 alongside Fidel Castro. Here are their speeches on the victory by Cuban, Angolan, and Namibian combatants over the US-backed South African army that had invaded Angola. $10. Also in Spanish and Farsi.

Marianas in Combat

Teté Puebla and the Mariana Grajales Women's Platoon in Cuba's Revolutionary War 1956–58

TETÉ PUEBLA

Brigadier General Teté Puebla, the highest ranking woman in Cuba's Revolutionary Armed Forces, joined the struggle to overthrow the US-backed dictatorship of Fulgencio Batista in 1956, when she was fifteen years old. This is her story—from clandestine action in the cities, to serving as an officer in the victorious Rebel Army's first all-women's unit. The fight to transform the social and economic status of women in Cuba remains inseparable from its socialist revolution. $14. Also in Spanish and Farsi.

Puerto Rico: Independence Is a Necessity

RAFAEL CANCEL MIRANDA

One of the five Puerto Rican Nationalists imprisoned by Washington for more than 25 years and released in 1979 speaks out on the brutal reality of US colonial domination, the campaign to free Puerto Rican political prisoners, the example of Cuba's socialist revolution, and the ongoing struggle for independence. $6. Also in Spanish and Farsi.

What Is to Be Done?

V.I. LENIN

The stakes in creating a disciplined organization of working-class revolutionaries capable of acting as a "tribune of the people, able to react to every manifestation of tyranny and oppression, no matter where it appears, to clarify for all and everyone the world-historic significance of the struggle for the emancipation of the proletariat." Written in 1902. In *Essential Works of Lenin.* $12.95

The Transitional Program for Socialist Revolution

LEON TROTSKY

Contains discussions between leaders of the US Socialist Workers Party and exiled revolutionary Leon Trotsky in 1938. The product of these discussions, a program of immediate, democratic, and transitional demands, was adopted by the SWP later that year. This program for socialist revolution remains a fighting guide for communist workers today. $20. Also in Farsi.

Fighting Racism in World War II

FROM THE PAGES OF THE *MILITANT*

An account of struggles against racist discrimination in US war industries, the armed forces, and society as a whole from 1939 to 1945, taken from the pages of the socialist newsweekly, the *Militant.* These struggles helped lay the basis for the proletarian-based civil rights movement that followed. $25

Teamster Bureaucracy

FARRELL DOBBS

How class-conscious workers led labor opposition to US imperialism's entry into World War II. And how Washington, aided by the Teamster bureaucracy, used the FBI to try to smash union power and gag antiwar views. Now with more than 130 photos and illustrations. $19. Also in Spanish.

Letters from Prison

JAMES P. CANNON

The prison letters of a communist leader, jailed for his party's opposition to the US imperialist war effort in World War II. Cannon discusses organizing a revolutionary party in wartime and preparing its postwar political course. $25

U.S. Imperialism Has Lost the Cold War

JACK BARNES

The collapse of regimes across Eastern Europe and the USSR claiming to be communist did not mean workers and farmers there had been crushed. In today's sharpening capitalist conflicts and wars, these toilers are an intractable obstacle to the profit system's advance, gaining leadership experience as they fight. In *New International* no. 11. $16. Also in Spanish, French, Farsi, and Greek.

The History of the Russian Revolution

LEON TROTSKY

The social, economic, and political dynamics of the first victorious socialist revolution as told by one of its central leaders. How, under Lenin's leadership, the Bolshevik Party led millions of workers and farmers to overthrow the state power of the landlords and capitalists in 1917 and bring to power a government that advanced their class interests at home and worldwide. Unabridged, 3 vols. in one. $38. Also in French and Russian.

To See the Dawn

Baku, 1920—First Congress of the Peoples of the East

How can peasants and workers in the colonial world achieve freedom from imperialist exploitation? By what means can working people overcome divisions incited by their national ruling classes and act together for their common class interests? These questions were addressed by 2,000 delegates to the 1920 Congress of the Peoples of the East. $24

Maurice Bishop Speaks

The Grenada Revolution and Its Overthrow, 1979–83

The triumph of the 1979 revolution in the Caribbean island of Grenada under the leadership of Maurice Bishop gave hope to millions throughout the Americas. Invaluable lessons from the workers and farmers government defeated by a Stalinist-led coup in 1983. $25

Lenin's Struggle for a Revolutionary International

Documents, 1907–1916; The Preparatory Years

The debate among revolutionary working-class leaders, including V.I. Lenin and Leon Trotsky, on a socialist response to World War I. $38

Revolutionary Continuity

Marxist Leadership in the United States

FARRELL DOBBS

"Successive generations of proletarian revolutionists have participated in the movements of the working class and its allies and sought to steer them along the correct path. . . . Marxists today owe them not only homage for their deeds. We also have a duty to learn where they went wrong as well as what they did right so their errors are not repeated."

—*Farrell Dobbs*

2 volumes: *The Early Years, 1848–1917,* $16; *Birth of the Communist Movement, 1918–1922,* $16.

PATHFINDER AROUND THE WORLD

Visit our website for a complete list of titles and to place orders

www.pathfinderpress.com

PATHFINDER DISTRIBUTORS

UNITED STATES

(and Caribbean, Latin America, and East Asia)

Pathfinder Books, 306 West 37th St., 13th Floor
New York, NY 10018

CANADA

Pathfinder Books, 7107 St. Denis, Suite 204
Montreal, QC H2S 2S5

UNITED KINGDOM

(and Europe, Africa, Middle East, and South Asia)

Pathfinder Books, 2nd Floor, 83 Kingsland High St.
Dalston, London E8 2PB

AUSTRALIA

(and Southeast Asia and the Pacific)

Pathfinder Books, Suite 22, 10 Bridge St.
Granville, NSW 2142

NEW ZEALAND

Pathfinder Books, 188a Onehunga Mall Rd., Onehunga, Auckland 1061
Postal address: P.O. Box 13857, Auckland 1643

Join the Pathfinder Readers Club
to get 15% discounts on all Pathfinder titles
and bigger discounts on special offers.
Sign up at www.pathfinderpress.com
or through the distributors above.
$10 a year